One Old Man Can't Be All That Bad

by
Ed O'Neal
with
David Bruce Murray

Copyright 2020 by Ed O'Neal

All rights reserved

Manufactured in the United States

O'Neal, Ed, 1936-

One Old Man Can't Be All That Bad

Reproduction and translation of any part of this book beyond the provisions permitted under the fair use guidelines of the US Copyright Law is a violation of federal law.

Table of Contents

Chapter One: My Big Break 1

Chapter Two: Growing Up 9

Chapter Three: Family Life 17

Chapter Four: Early Music Groups 25

Chapter Five: From Fill-In to Owner 33

Chapter Six: It Starts with a Song 47

Chapter Seven: The DMB Band 55

Chapter Eight: Return to Traditional Quartet 65

Chapter Nine: Ed O'Neal University 87

Chapter Ten: Joy O'Neal 107

Chapter Eleven: Awards and Testimonials 115

Chapter Twelve: Road Stories 147

FOREWARD

One Old Man Can't Be All That Bad may seem like a strange title for the autobiography of Ed O'Neal. Ed is one of Southern Gospel's living legends after all. He has owned the Dixie Melody Boys since the 1960s, and he was inducted into the Southern Gospel Music Association's Hall of Fame in 2004. I will explain why we chose this title.

The phrase comes from the chorus of the Dixie Melody Boys' song "Antioch Church Choir" which was a number one hit for the group in 1982. Almost forty years later, the story of an old man who could not pass the audition to sing in the church choir is still a signature song for the Dixie Melody Boys.

If you get to talk to Ed for more than a few minutes, you will quickly discover his love for the game of golf. Ed and the late bass singer Rex Nelon played many rounds over the years.

After the Dixie Melody Boys struck gold with "Antioch Church Choir," Ed said Rex would often sing that line "one old man can't be all that bad" to him on the golf course as a joke. McCray Dove who sang lead for the Dixie Melody Boys for many years recalled the fun those two bass singers had with that line and suggested it as the title for Ed's book. So, the book title is not merely a line from a song; it is also a tip of the hat to Rex Nelon and the time he and Ed enjoyed on the golf course.

I have observed Ed O'Neal from a distance and been a fan for the past twenty-five years or so. I remember seeing the Dixie

Melody Boys sing at a big Southern Gospel day at the Carowinds theme park near Charlotte, North Carolina back in the 1990s. Harold Reed was singing tenor by that point, so it was probably in 1994 or so. They really got the place wound up on the last song. McCray Dove came off the stage into the crowd and when they finished, he didn't rejoin the group. Instead, he went up through the crowd yelling "Woo" every few seconds as the emcee was introducing the next group!

As the years went by, I got to know McCray and some of the other guys who passed through the Dixie Melody Boys on their way to other groups. I had met Ed's longtime bus driver, Rayburn Lane, but I had never met Ed himself. A few months ago, McCray Dove called me and asked if I had any interest in helping Ed put his life's story into book form. My answer was an enthusiastic, "YES!" I couldn't wait to get started on his book.

What a joy it has been to have Ed O'Neal visit in my home. I've sat and listened to him talk for hours about all the highs and lows of owning a quartet and singing full-time. Most of the time, I found myself laughing at his hilarious road stories. We saved that chapter for last!

Thank you, Ed, for the opportunity to translate your amazing life into book form. It has been a delight.

May God continue to bless you!
David Bruce Murray
July 10, 2020

Chapter One: My Big Break

I'll explain all the circumstances surrounding my start in life later, but first, I want to tell you how the Dixie Melody Boys and I, Ed O'Neal, were able to transform from a small gospel quartet that sang in eastern North Carolina to one that traveled all over the United States and Canada.

My wife Joy and I took a vacation trip to the National Quartet Convention in 1970. My baritone singer and his wife went with us, and the car we traveled in was a Mercury. I was living in Kinston, North Carolina at this time, but the day we left I first had to go to Raleigh real early for a business meeting at 8:00 AM.

I'm not sure what time we finally got on the road, but it was before lunch. This was before the interstate highway was built, so we took US 70 through Asheville and across into

Tennessee. That was a long haul on a two-lane road. We spent the night just on the other side of Nashville, and it was late at night when we got there. We drove on to Memphis for the convention the next day.

That trip happened to be the last year the convention was held in Memphis. It was held in the Ellis Auditorium, and boy, you better believe it really turned me on as a young gospel singer. That auditorium is gone now, but they've built the Cook Convention Center on the same site, and that's where they hold the Memphis Quartet Show now every June.

My wife and I and the other couple were just there as fans in the stands that first year we went. We didn't really meet anybody as far as the main groups. We were just there to enjoy the music. They had such a big crowd that the main auditorium was sold out. They also had a smaller auditorium where each group would sing again. If you liked the Thrasher Brothers, for example, you could see them in one room and then go over to the other auditorium to see them again.

All of that was thrilling to me.

The following year in 1971, the convention was moved to Nashville. Joy and I attended again that year as spectators.

On Saturday, they had what they called a "Semi-Pro Parade." If you were an amateur group, you could come and sing two songs. You weren't paid anything, but you got to sing in front of that crowd.

I looked at Joy and said, "Now, that's interesting. Next year, I'll bring my group and sing on that."

She said she thought that would be nice. We made our plans and our reservations to go back with the group in 1972.

The next year we couldn't hardly wait. I carried the group down there to sing that Saturday morning. I think we were still traveling in cars that year. I don't remember taking a bus on that trip. We weren't full-time at that point.

I can't remember exactly what two songs we sang, but it had to be something like "I'd Rather Be an Old-Time Christian" or something in a similar upbeat style. Whatever it was, we got on there for two songs, and boy, that crowd went crazy. They just really enjoyed the kind of songs we were singing. The response was more than I could ever imagine.

After it was over, we had lunch and rested for a bit. Then, that afternoon we went back early and walked around in the memorial hall there to see all the displays that were set up. Joy and I were just walking when I felt a big arm come around my shoulder.

I looked up and it was JD Sumner.

I almost fainted.

JD was my hero, but I had never met him before. I should also mention that the reason the convention had moved from Memphis to Nashville in 1971 was because that was the first year that JD and JD alone owned the event. He bought out his partners the previous year, and so it was his sole decision to move it to Nashville. Not only was I meeting my hero, I was meeting the top man in charge of the convention!

As I was still realizing who it was that had walked up and put his arm on my shoulder, he said in that big full voice of his, "Boy, you really like this, don't you?"

He saw something in me.

I said, "Yeah, I do, I really do."

JD said, "Well, I'll tell you what. You bring that little group back down here next year and I'll put you on the big stage."

I said, "When would you want me to sing?"

He said, "When I tell you to!"

I've been going to the quartet convention ever since.

Even more importantly, the man who had been my hero for so long grew to be my pal. We were friends from the moment that happened until he passed away. JD and I played golf together, and we talked often for the rest of his life. We sure enjoyed a lot of laughs.

Singing at the National Quartet Convention opened doors for the Dixie Melody Boys to go other places. One of these was an annual event in Lansdale, Pennsylvania put on by the Couriers, the Jacobs Brothers, and the Eastmen.

After we went to the convention, I got a call and was invited to bring the Dixie Melody Boys up there to sing. I'd never been that far from home other than the trip to Memphis, but we loaded up and took about the same amount of product we'd take to a concert close to home. Man, we sold everything we had on the bus, and I knew then we'd be coming back to Pennsylvania. That state is one of my favorite places to sing to this day.

The Jacobs Brothers kept that concert going annually. They moved it to a location in Dillsburg, Pennsylvania called the King's Kids Campground where they'd have kids out for a week at a time. We went back to that event for forty to forty-five years. Groups like the Cathedrals came in. Pretty much everybody worked that event. In fact, this past year was the final year the Jacobs Brothers oversaw that concert.

That first trip to Pennsylvania is where I met Ed Knox. He lived in California and promoted concerts out there, but he'd married a girl from Pennsylvania and was at the concert that night. That meeting later led to us going on a tour to the west coast once a year. We'd do two or three weeks out there.

On one of those trips, we had a date in Lebanon, Oregon that the Knox Brothers put together. When we got there, Ed Knox said they had another group on the program that night. It was JD Sumner & the Stamps Quartet. They'd had a cancellation and just wanted to come sing. Well, we had a great time that night and from then on, every time we went to the west coast, we'd do about six or seven dates with JD and the Stamps. That was a lot of fun.

One day we were doing a date in Seattle, Washington when JD was with us, and both groups had to go over into British Columbia across the Canadian border for the next date. JD was riding in a 45-foot Eagle and I had a 40-foot Eagle at the time. We were sitting there on the bus, and I said, "JD, we gotta go into British Columbia tomorrow."

He said, "Yeah, I know."

I said, "I tell you what I've been doing. To keep from having to take all my merchandise and declare it at the border, I've been renting a motel room on this side of the border. I put most of my merchandise in there, go do the concert in Canada, come back to get my stuff, and take off."

I said, "But I've got an idea.

JD said, "What's that?"

I said, "Why don't we take one of our buses and put all the merchandise on it and all of us go on the other bus?"

JD said, "Well, you ain't as dumb as I thought you was. I guess you want to go on mine, too."

I said, "Well, yours is 45-foot. You've got a little more room."

So that's what we did.

We also worked on the west coast with people like Herb Henry in Modesto, Ralph Dean in the Los Angeles area, and Gary Young in Bakersville.

The old school was different, you know. The atmosphere was different. There was more fellowship between groups back then, and you were accepted more. The Dixie Melody Boys were a brand-new group, but some of the more established groups became our buddies.

Meeting JD and the circumstances of when I met him at that first Nashville convention was a big moment in my career and the early years of the Dixie Melody Boys. Up until then, we were regional.

Now, we thought we were singing a whole lot, but we just covered North Carolina and some parts of Virginia back then. We had stayed busy and developed a following in our area. There were no auditoriums around town we couldn't fill, but we weren't known more than 100 miles or so from home.

Everybody had jobs. We could not leave until we all got off work on Friday. We'd take off and sing Friday night, Saturday night, and Sunday. It was a rare event if we ever went as far as South Carolina.

You see, one thing led to another. Those first two trips to the National Quartet Convention with my wife Joy are what led to me going back and taking the group to sing on the amateur stage. Doing well on the small amateur stage led to us moving to sing on the big stage in the years after that. It all really made me see there was a whole new world out there.

Not only did I meet my hero when I took my group for the first time, it was a big turning point in my life at the time with regards to moving the Dixie Melody Boys from a regional group to a national group. I'll have more JD stories to tell later in this book, but for now, I just wanted to focus on that initial meeting.

I miss him.

Chapter Two: Growing Up

I was born on May 28, 1936 in a little town called Fuquay-Varina, North Carolina. I don't remember anything about it, of course, because I was an infant. I really don't know much about Fuquay-Varina at all, as a matter of fact.

We moved to Raleigh, the capital city of North Carolina, when I was very small, and that's where I have all my earliest memories. I don't remember a time that I ever went back to the town of my birth. Rayburn Lane, my long-time bus driver, says he has been there, but I don't believe I've ever been back.

My daddy's name was Jones Eural O'Neal, but everyone called my daddy "JE." He owned a couple of dump trucks back in those days and was just trying to eke out a living. The country was still in the middle of the Great Depression when I was born.

One story I remember my daddy telling was about buying some tires on credit for his trucks. When he couldn't pay for them on time, they came out and jacked up his trucks and took the tires back. Times were hard for everybody in those days.

Both of my parents were regular church-going people for as long as I can remember. My mother's name was Lottie Jones O'Neal. She taught my brothers and me to sing harmony.

I was the "baby" of the family, the youngest of three brothers. My middle brother, Lynn, was two years older than me, and my oldest brother, Louis, was about 13 months older than Lynn, so approximately three years older than me.

We moved around several times. My first memories are from a place where we lived in the suburbs of Raleigh. Blue Ridge Boulevard was one of the main roads where the State Fair was held. Our house was down a road, or really, I should say it was more of a path off of that street.

The next place we moved was closer to downtown in a house on Hargett Street. I remember the house was high enough off the ground that I played under it with my cars and toys. I was still just a toddler at that point.

After I got a little older, we lived in a federal housing project. It was called Halifax Court Apartments. In the meantime, my daddy had got a job with Carolina Trailways. I remember he made a statement to my mama that he felt like he could pay every bill he had with that first check. Back then, it was a little above the average income. We remained at that location until I finished the fifth grade.

The job with Carolina Trailways enabled my daddy to save enough money to buy a piece of land on Leesville Road, right off Durham Highway, not far from Raleigh-Durham Airport. He rented a house there and we started building on that property he bought. All the labor on the new house was done by him and the three of us boys. I don't think there was a square wall in the house, but we made it!

I'll tell you about one of my memories of my granddaddy from back in the old days. People used to go to each other's house on Sundays to sit in the yard and visit, you know. People don't do that no more.

I remember being at my granddaddy's house one day not long after they had put a telephone in. They'd never had a telephone, but the kids wanted them to have it so they could check in on them. We were sitting out in the yard and that phone went to ringing. I said, "Granddaddy, the phone is ringing."

He said, "I hear it, but I don't know a soul that I need to talk to."

Granddaddy just wasn't too concerned about answering the phone. When I compare that way of life to now, I sometimes wonder if everything that has happened with technology is really an improvement. Whoever is calling or texting on the phone always seems to be more important than anything else that might be happening in the same room with you.

Our new address was on Cary Rural Route 1, and I started sixth grade at the elementary school there in Cary. I probably shouldn't tell this, but I caught up with my middle brother Lynn. He'd been held back.

Cary Elementary was on the same campus as Cary High School, which is where I graduated in 1955. I was still a student there at Cary High when I started my first job working for a company called NC Products. They made concrete drainage pipes. I worked there a couple of years.

Cary High was also where I met my future wife Joy. Well, I should be more accurate and say the first time Joy saw me was some years earlier when I was singing with my brothers, but I'll tell all about that in another chapter of this book.

I joined the National Guard when I was a senior in high school. The Korean War had ended in 1953, but military service was still an important thing in the 1950s just a few years removed from World War II. Some people called us "draft dodgers" because we joined the National Guard, but I was in there for one full term which I think was five years at that time.

Initially there were training meetings once a week. I was in the air division of the National Guard, so our meetings were at the airport there in Raleigh. Later we were just required to go to meetings once per month, but for those, we'd drive to Fort Bragg and stay for a weekend.

I also went to a business college in Raleigh called King's Business College. I took a course in accounting and worked for a while after that as a bookkeeper in a warehouse.

My father had been born in 1907 and was a few years older than my mother. He was in his late seventies when he passed away in 1986. My mother lived an even longer life passing away at the age of 97 in 2010.

One of my sweetest remembrances of my mother happened when she was living in a retirement village. We gave her a little Christmas party, and I was sitting beside her on the couch. I said, "Mother, let's sing some Christmas songs."

She said, "Oh, I can't sing no more."

I said, "Yeah, you can."

I was holding her hand and started singing "Silent Night" and she started harmonizing on it. Water just flew in my eyes. She still had that voice.

It was weak, but she was right on pitch. After she passed away, she was buried beside my father at Brier Creek Memorial Gardens cemetery in Raleigh.

I am so grateful to have been raised in a Christian home and for two parents who were able to get me started down the right path in life.

A young and skinny Ed O'Neal at Christmas!

Chapter Three: Family Life

Before I met my wife, Joy, I was kind of sweet on another girl. The O'Neal Trio (my two brothers and I) went to sing at Westover Elementary School which was where Joy and this other girl attended at the time. This other girl came to hear us sing and kind of flirt with me, and she had brought my future wife Joy with her. Joy was in the eighth grade at that time.

They didn't have a high school on the Westover campus like we did at Cary, so after Joy finished eighth grade, she came to high school at Cary High. That was when Joy and I really got to noticing each other and started courting.

Our first date was going fishing on a double date with my brother Lynn and another girl. Joy and I dated quite a while, and of course, we were still in school for most of it. Back then, long courtships were common. I guess we dated close to three or four years.

We had gone over to her sister's house one night and we were playing cards; it was probably spades or something like that. Her sister's husband looked at us and said, "When in the world are y'all going to get married? You've been dating so long."

I said, "Just deal the cards, man. We're going to get married the fourth of July. Deal."

Now, I was just joking, but two weeks later, Joy went and put her engagement picture in the newspaper. The date was set for the fourth of July. It kind of shocked me at the time, but it sure did turn out all right.

We were married on July 4, 1956. One thing led to another, and it lasted sixty years!

After our wedding, Joy and I rented a little duplex on West Cabarrus Street in Raleigh. We were still living there when our first son was born almost two years later on May 26, 1958. We named him Edward Allen O'Neal Jr. and called him Allen.

The next place where Joy and I moved was out on the edge of the Raleigh city limits. It was a little two-bedroom house that we rented from a man named Mr. Talbot. Allen was a just little tot when we moved there.

We stayed at that location until we bought our first home in a subdivision that was just across the street from the Raleigh Golf Association's course. We were living in the subdivision when our second son was born on July 3, 1961. We named him Ralph Winstead O'Neal, but we always called him "Randy."

When they got older, I took both of my sons on the road with me. Allen stuck with it and is still making music today with a group called Jackson Heights. I'll tell you more about them in a later chapter.

Randy decided that traveling and making music just wasn't for him. He had a very successful career in the military rising to the rank of Lieutenant Colonel before he retired three years ago, and then he went to work with the US Department of Agriculture. He never has told me how much he makes, but he ought to be doing pretty good. He travels a lot for his job. He called me from Brownsville, Texas not long ago.

By the mid-1960s, we had moved again to a project called Pinehurst Park in Garner, NC just outside of Raleigh. We were living there when our daughter Dara Marie O'Neal, "the princess," was born on February 17, 1965. Dara is a nurse now and an excellent photographer, too.

I was selling real estate at this point while we were living in Garner, and I did well for a while. By 1966, I had some houses built, but then the market took a downturn and I couldn't sell anything.

I had a friend who loved gospel music and loved to hear us sing. He owned a business in Cary, North Carolina called Taylor Biscuit Company. They sold snack foods like cookies, peanuts, crackers, and chips. Their biggest competitor was Lance. I went to see him about getting a job, and he said, "Ed, we really don't have anything available right now, but let's go down the hall and talk to the sales manager."

So, we did. The man's name was Mr. Barnes, one of the finest men I ever met, and he made a job for me. When I went back home, I got out of the building business. I just turned it over to one of the superintendents working for me, and I never looked back on that.

I worked for Taylor Biscuit for a few years as a troubleshooter. I traveled town to town and state to state checking inventory behind route men. After some time doing this and building up the territory, I took a manager's position down in Kinston, North Carolina, which is the town where I live now.

I was really enjoying that, and we moved over to Kinston in 1968. Taylor Biscuit had been a small company when I started. Their route men would call on the smaller mom-and-pop type stores, but I began getting them into some of the larger chain stores like A&P and so forth.

They called me one morning and told me I needed to come to Raleigh for a sales meeting on a certain date. I said, "Brother, I can't do that. We're starting our vacation then."

This was in 1970, the week my wife and I had planned our vacation trip to Memphis for the National Quartet Convention that I described in the first chapter of this book. He said, "Well, you've got no choice. You've got to be here."

I said, "No, I can't do it. We've already made plans and reservations, and I've got another couple going with me."

They relented some and asked, "What time are you coming through Raleigh?"

I told him, and we compromised and had the meeting early in the morning around 8:00 AM, so I could attend with the rest of the managers and then be on my way to Memphis.

When I arrived at the meeting, they had a big map on the wall. This was the sort of company that didn't ask for your opinion before they made a decision. They just told you what they had decided you were going to do. In this meeting they said, "Ed, we're moving you from Kinston, North Carolina to manage Norfolk, Virginia."

My boss looked at me to see my reaction and I tried my best to look normal. After the meeting he asked if I was going to move to Norfolk, and I said, "Well, that's what they said."

I had built the sales up around Kinston, which is why they wanted me to move and do the same thing in Norfolk. Rather than moving the family away from Kinston, though, I started staying in a motel in Norfolk. I would work all week and then come home to see my family on the weekends.

In the meantime, Taylor Biscuit was sold to Omaha Foods, the company that makes Austin crackers. After some time had passed, the big man from Omaha Foods, Mr. Jones, called me one day and said he was on his way to Norfolk and asked me to pick him up at the airport on the 11:00 AM flight. I said that I would. Keep in mind, I was staying there at the Holiday Inn in Norfolk.

I'd never met Mr. Jones. When I picked him up, he asked if we could go get lunch. Then he asked if the Holiday Inn there had a good restaurant. I told him it did and brought him back to the motel where I had been staying. See, he already knew more about me than he was letting on. We talked for a bit and then he looked at me and said, "You're not gonna move here, are you?"

I said, "No sir."

He said, "I didn't think so. Well man, I sure hate to lose you. You've done a fantastic job for us."

Then he shook my hand and wished me well.

So, I went back home and opened a carpet shop at the plaza in Kinston called Fashion Carpets. I ran that business for a few years and eventually sold it to one of my salesmen.

I had already bought the Dixie Melody Boys by this time, although at some points along the way, I had to put them on hold due to the time I had to focus on earning a living first with Taylor Biscuit and later with the carpet store.

I've already told you about my family life growing up, where we lived, how I met my wife Joy, and my early professional career. In the next chapter, I'm going to take you all the way back to my childhood again and explain just how my music career came to be.

Chapter Four: Early Music Groups

When I was four years old, I received my first love offering for singing a song. It happened at Mount Olivet Baptist Church, which was our family's home church on Blue Ridge Boulevard in Raleigh. I guess we started attending there shortly after moving to the little house off Blue Ridge Boulevard, which was before I was old enough to remember living anywhere else.

They stood me up in a chair beside the pulpit and gave me the OK to sing the Jimmie Davis song, "You Are My Sunshine." In the love offering, I was given a nickel, a pack of Juicy Fruit chewing gum, and a plastic pocketknife. I wish I had kept that pocketknife.

My mother's family was all singers. They all could sing very well, and it was a big family. I'd go with them when they would sing in churches almost every weekend. It just thrilled me to death to go with them. My mother had nine brothers and there were two sisters; eleven in total. By the time they all got married, with the in-laws, they made a big choir! That's one of my earliest remembrances of hearing good singing.

It wasn't just a hobby to them. They were big-time singers. They even had a guy come in to tutor them.

It was my mother who taught my brothers Louis and Lynn and me to sing harmony. We were called the O'Neal Trio and had a regular program on WRAL-AM radio every Saturday morning at 9:00 AM. Fred Fletcher and his brother owned that radio station, and we were very young when we started. This was around the time my family was living at Halifax Court Apartments in Raleigh.

As a kid, I had no idea how important that was to be heard on radio. The O'Neal Trio got invitations to go places I wouldn't have hardly believed. My daddy wasn't a singer, but he acted as our booking agent. Sometimes he had us out singing when we'd have rather been doing something else.

Back in those days about every weekend, there was a Sunday afternoon gospel singing somewhere, either in a big church or a high school. I sang first tenor, and the other groups around there hated me!

These quartets would show up with their fancy suits and ties, and here a little guy like me would come with his two brothers. I was singing stuff like "I'm A Bible Loving Man" real high, and it would just tear the people up. That was my sugar stick. I had a high squeaky voice, but all the people loved it because I was just a kid. Those quartet boys didn't want to follow a little kid that could sing that way. They'd see me coming and say, "You ain't got no business being here."

When we were still singing, we made an acetate recording on a machine that somebody had in their living room. Boy, I sure do wish I could find a copy of that to listen to again. That brings back good memories. My brothers and I sang as the O'Neal Trio for several years until my brothers left for military service.

After they got out of singing, I continued to sing in various other settings. The Trailways station where my daddy JE O'Neal worked as a bus driver was directly across the road from Pennington-Smith Funeral Home. He knew all those guys at the funeral home and prompted them to ask me to sing whenever they needed music for a funeral. I ended up singing there quite often while looking down on someone in the coffin that I didn't even know. I didn't enjoy doing this at all. I finally said, "Dad, don't make me do that no more."

As I became a teenager, my voice was changing, and my daddy didn't want me to sing. I'm not sure what he based his theory on, but he believed you could damage your voice if you sang too much while your voice was in the process of changing. So, for approximately two years, he forbid me to sing.

After my voice settled in the bass range, I started a new group called the Gospel Harmony Quartet. This group was formed after I married my wife Joy in 1956, but I can't remember the exact year.

The members of the Gospel Harmony Quartet included my mother's youngest brother William Jones singing lead, Cliff Pleasants on tenor, a cousin of mine named Jimmy Jones on baritone (this was not the same Jimmy Jones who sang bass with the LeFevres), me singing bass, and Joe Walker at the piano.

We did it just for enjoyment, but we got fairly busy singing locally. We recorded one LP. I probably still have a copy of it at my house in storage somewhere.

I bought a used limousine from a funeral home in Raleigh for us to travel to our concerts. It was low mileage, and I thought that made us look like a first-class group when we'd arrive in that big car.

This was when I was still in the National Guard, so I'd also drive the limo to Fort Bragg for our meetings. If any other boys from our area wanted to ride with me, I'd charge them five dollars apiece so they wouldn't have to drive their own cars. Back in them days, five dollars was a lot of money.

After that, I joined a group called the Serenaders Quartet. They had been full-time in the past. Vern Sullivan who wrote the famous song "Rainbow Avenue" for Palmetto State Quartet and Buddy Burton were going to college in Buies Creek, North Carolina, which is not far from Fayetteville. They wanted to get the Serenaders Quartet going again and they called to ask me to sing bass. Gerald Milligan who had been with the group before played piano and sang tenor. I agreed to do it, because I wanted to sing and felt like it was a step up in terms of the overall talent.

The Serenaders made one album while I was with them. It had a pretty hand-painted cover that was maroon in color with a white bible. The title was *If You Know The Lord*.

That was my first time singing with Buddy Burton. He was a mess then and he is still a mess today. Preachers loved him, too, because he was always joking around. I guess I have known Buddy longer than most anyone else in the singing business.

All this experience was preparing me for something bigger, although I didn't know it at the time. After my time with the Serenaders, I was going to join the group that I would later own.

It would become my life's work.

Gospel Harmony Quartet – (left to right) Ed O'Neal, Joe Walker, William Jones (Ed's uncle), Cliff Pleasants, and Jimmy Jones (Ed's cousin)

Cover image of the only recording made by the Serenaders Quartet while Ed O'Neal was a member of the group

Serenaders Quartet – Buddy Burton, Gerald Milligan, Ed O'Neal, and Vern Sullivan

Chapter Five: From Fill-In to Owner

I don't really know all the history of the Dixie Melody Boys before I arrived. This group formed around 1960, but there were several other groups that used the name before that time.

In fact, I was in the office one day and the phone rang. I picked it up and it was someone at a radio station. They said, "Ed, we're cleaning out the inventory down here and we found a 78-rpm record of the Dixie Melody Boys."

I said, "No, that's a mistake somewhere. We never made anything on 78-rpm. We don't go that far back."

She said, "Well, we've got it if you want it."

I went down there and got it, and it was good singing! It was like something the Swanee River Boys might have done; you know that little bumpy singing they used to do. They really were good, and the label on that 78 said those Dixie Melody Boys were from Arkansas.

I don't think there was any connection between those Dixie Melody Boys and my group. The Dixie Melody Boys I joined and eventually came to own was formed by Avis Adkins around 1960. Avis initially called the group the Helmsmen, but that word was too hard for people to understand on the telephone. If Avis called a promoter, he would have to repeat the name several times before it was understood.

The man who is helping me put this book together researched it and found out that Avis Adkins had a cousin named Asbury Adkins who had managed a Dixie Melody Boys group back in the 1950s. After Avis realized the Helmsmen name wasn't working, he contacted his cousin Asbury and got permission to use the Dixie Melody Boys name.

Along with Avis singing lead, the other group members of that original group were Buddy Hawley singing bass, Ralph Walker singing tenor, Gene Payne singing baritone, and a kid named Tony Brown playing piano. They were part-time, but they had a lot of local fans supporting them.

After some time, Marvin Harris joined the group to sing bass, replacing Buddy Hawley. Marvin was a truck driver. After he'd been with the group for a while, his company required him to relocate too far away for him to continue singing.

I can't remember every detail of my early history with the Dixie Melody Boys. I think I joined them first in 1963, but I'm not 100% positive that was the year. I do remember I was still singing with the Serenaders when Avis Adkins called and asked if I would come sing bass. This was when I was building houses and selling real estate, and I was so busy I just didn't think I had any more time to spare.

I explained the situation to Avis. I told him I would sing, but only as a fill-in until he could find somebody else to sing bass. I expected I would sing with them for a few weeks until Avis could find someone else to take over, but he never did.

I guess you might say I've been filling in ever since!

Later, I came to own and manage the group. We were on our way to Wilmington, North Carolina one day to sing with the Oak Ridge Boys and a discussion started on the bus about the group's finances. I stayed out of it, because I was still just a fill-in, not a full-fledged member of the group. It didn't get out of hand or anything, but the discussion got a little heavy.

One of them asked me, "Ed, what would you do?

I said, "Oh, leave me out of it, boys, I'm not part of this."

Avis pressed me, "Well, if you were part of it, what would you do?"

I told him how I would handle the situation, and that led to him offering me the option of buying them out. We agreed on a price. I had some legal papers drawn up by my lawyer, Sam Johnson, who I used for my real estate transactions. That's how I came to own the Dixie Melody Boys.

I've always thought that original group was pretty tough. We still had Tony Brown at the piano. He was just a kid at the time, but he already had the kind of talent that made people sit up and notice.

In fact, when Tony left to go to the Stamps-Baxter school that was held every year at Murray State University in Kentucky back in those days, I had a feeling he wouldn't be back. I was right. After that trip, Tony joined the Trav'lers Quartet for a short time, then he joined the Klaudt Indian Family. He later went on to play for JD Sumner & The Stamps Quartet where he got the nickname "Tarzan."

Now, let me take a detour for a minute to tell you about my salvation experience, because it happened around this time and that is the most important thing that ever happened in my life.

My family attended Mount Olivet Baptist Church on Blue Ridge Boulevard in Raleigh when I was a child as I mentioned in a previous chapter. Even after we moved around in Raleigh, we kept attending that church. I can't remember exactly how old I was when I joined the church and was baptized. It might have been at the end of a week of Vacation Bible School. I just want to be clear when I say that I only joined the church at that time. I wasn't really saved.

It wasn't until I was around 28 years old and had moved to Garner, North Carolina and was building houses that I had my true salvation experience. Things weren't good financially for me at that time. I was going through a lot, but I'd been attending a church there in Garner called Hayes Chapel Christian Church. That's where I really accepted Christ. They emphasized a salvation message there and I responded to it. You can be a good person all your life, but if you don't accept Christ, you're not really saved.

During this period, I bought the assets of the Dixie Melody Boys, but there were a few times my work forced me to put the group on hold. After I moved to Kinston, some of my old buddies that knew me from singing wanted to get together and sing again. I said, "No, I don't have time right now. I've got too much going on."

They kept insisting, "Let's just sing a couple of times each month."

Well, you can't do that. Once you start singing and the people like you, they're going to invite you to keep coming, so we got it started back up after my job with Taylor Biscuit ended. I was settled in Kinston by that point, and I had opened up a carpet store. It was overwhelming at times. Sometimes a member of the Dixie Melody Boys would run the carpet store for a day just so I could get a little break.

I had always considered the group to be a part-time thing up to that point. I just couldn't branch out too far if I was also having to be involved in something like real estate, or working for Taylor Biscuit Company, or running a carpet store. If I was going to sing full-time, I had to step out on faith.

I was sitting there at the carpet shop one day and thought about how much I'd rather be singing than messing with that other stuff. I just HAD to do it, and I made up my mind I was going to give it a shot. I sold the carpet shop soon after that to one of my salesmen, and the rest is history.

I had always wanted to sing. From the first time I saw the Florida Boys march out on stage with orange suits on, it did something to me. They were IT in that day and time, and I just wanted to do the same type of thing. I felt like I had what it took as a singer. After all, I had been singing my entire life, and I also had experience by that point working with people in various businesses.

It was during the mid-1970s that we became a full-time group. When I told the guys in the group what I had decided, not all of them felt like they could give up their jobs to give it a go as a full-time group. We had some changes in the line-up.

I first brought in a tenor singer named Jimmy Jones from Virginia. This was yet another Jimmy Jones, not my cousin Jimmy Jones who had sung baritone in my old group or the bass singer who traveled with the LeFevres. Completing the group was Dewey Williams singing lead, and Henry Daniels singing baritone.

I've been blessed with the ability to make friends. When you go full-time, you'd better have some contacts. I got on the phone and started lining up dates.

Jimmy Jones was only with us a short time. I then hired a young man named Jamey Ragle to sing tenor. I had met him in Ohio. He's a big evangelist now. He was the sort of person people remembered after they met him. He was a comedian really, a funny guy with a great personality.

After the exposure we had received appearing at the National Quartet Convention in the early 1970s, Wheeling Gospel Talent Agency began lining up dates for us to sing on fairs around the country and it just continued to balloon from there. Around this time, our lead singer Dewey Williams decided to leave. We were working at 20 or 30 fairs per year, and it was a rather stressful period for everyone.

One of the best singers I ever hired was our next lead singer. His name was David Kimbrell. We were out on the road when Dewey resigned. I called David and asked him to come from Florida up to where we were in Morgantown, West Virginia. We recorded several albums with him. David turned out to be a great preacher, too. He just retired not long ago.

The best-selling album we recorded in the late 1970s was on the Queen City Albums (QCA) label. The album was titled *Sending Up Some Boards* and the song by the same title was real good for us in those days. It was written by a preacher over in Kentucky named Eddie Isaacs. We recorded another one of his songs later called "Factory Recall." They were unusual songs, but they were catchy. We were nominated for a Grammy award on that *Sending Up Some Boards* album. You talk about a tickled man. They sent me a roll of stickers to put on the album covers with that little dog sitting in front of a record player. Of course, this was before "Antioch Church Choir."

George Younce and Glen Payne were special to me through those early years. You can't do this kind of work without help. I've been blessed, and I'll be honest with you, I've enjoyed it. I don't feel like a man is ever really successful until he finds something to do that he really enjoys.

George and I were talking one day, and he said, "You know, Gospel music is a rather unique thing that we do. It's not enough if you just like it. You've got to have a real passion for it."

Any of the successful groups you saw, whether it be the Blackwood Brothers or JD and them or whoever, they had a passion for it. When the money didn't come in, they weren't happy about it, but they were still out there. They had a passion for it.

I can honestly say I had that passion.

In fact, I still do. I would still be out there if my health would allow me to travel.

*Dixie Melody Boys (1960s before Ed O'Neal joined the group)
(back row left to right) Marvin Harris, Ralph Walker, Gene Payne
(front row left to right) Avis Adkins, Tony Brown*

*Early album recorded by the Dixie Melody Boys before Ed O'Neal joined
(left to right) Ralph Walker, Avis Adkins, Marvin Harris, Tony Brown, Gene Payne*

Dixie Melody Boys (partly)
(back row left to right) a good friend Ellis Jones, Delmar Tilghman, Ralph Walker, Ralph Walker's cousin, Everette Harper, Ed O'Neal
(front row left to right) two unidentified boys

1973 album
(left to right) Charles Forehand, Everett Harper, Delmar Tilghman, John Jarman, Jerry Dunbar, Ed O'Neal

Early-1970s Dixie Melody Boys in the studio
(left to right behind unidentified studio musician) John Jarman, Delmar Tilghman, Charles Forehand, Ed O'Neal, Everett Harper

1970s Dixie Melody Boys
(back row left to right) Ed O'Neal, Jamey Ragle, Ron Wells, Henry Daniels
(front row left to right) Reb Lancaster, Allen O'Neal, David Kimbrell, Greg Simpkins

1970s Dixie Melody Boys
(left to right) Ed O'Neal, Willie Ollinger, Ron Wells, Tom Jones, David Kimbrell, Reb Lancaster, Allen O'Neal, Jamey Ragle

1980 Dixie Melody Boys
(left to right) Phil Barker, David Kimbrell, Tom Jones, Ed O'Neal

1981 Dixie Melody Boys
(back row left to right) Phil Barker, Ed O'Neal, Allen O'Neal, Randy O'Neal
(front row left to right) David Kimbrell, Jerry Kelso, Frank Sutton, Ron Wells

Ed O'Neal with comedian Jerry Clower

Chapter Six: It Starts with a Song

I've dabbled with songwriting off and on, but I probably just have one I can honestly say was ever a hit. For a while, I had a Christian bookstore downtown in Kinston, and it was one of my days to be at the store. It was raining and storming outside, so we only had a few customers. I was just sitting in there scribbling words on my notepad.

I looked down and said, "Man, this looks like a song."

I kept on and put a tune to it and gave it the title "When I Cross to the Other Side of Jordan." The ironic thing was when I took it to my group, they didn't want to do it. They didn't think much about it, so I didn't press it.

I let Claude Hopper publish it and the Hopper Brothers & Connie were the ones that recorded it first in 1974. After that, the Inspirations recorded it and by that time, my boys were asking why I didn't let them record it first.

I said, "Because y'all didn't want to."

JD Sumner & the Stamps Quartet recorded it on their *Live at Murray State* album. That's my favorite recording of the song. The song has been recorded many times since then. I've lost count of how many groups have recorded it.

Kenna Turner West called me not too long ago and said she wanted to write an article about that song for *Singing News*. I told her I didn't think anybody would remember the song. She said, "Well, I do."

She wrote the story up for the March 2020 issue.

As I mentioned, I don't write many songs, but since then the Dixie Melody Boys have recorded a few of mine. I eventually let them record "When I Cross to the Other Side of Jordan" too. We've probably sung that song more than any other over the years.

We've mostly recorded songs written by other songwriters, though. Herman Harper sent me a song one day and said he thought it sounded like something the Dixie Melody Boys could do.

It was called "Antioch Church Choir" and was written by a guy named Darrell Holt. As soon as I heard it, I got excited and set a date for us to go to Nashville and cut a record for that song.

We recorded it at the studio that the Oak Ridge Boys owned on Rockland Road. Tony Brown who had played piano for us in the early 1960s came by while we were there. After we finished the vocals, Herman Harper and the guys were in there putting church bells on the track. Tony asked me if that was going to be our single, and I said that it was. He said, "You better hurry."

I said, "Why?"

He said, "I just finished a session with another group that is planning to send it out."

I told Herman we had to hurry if we wanted to be first getting it to radio. Herman said he'd have it on the market within two weeks. He was true to his word. "Antioch Church Choir" hit the charts and started climbing until it shot right up to the number one spot in September 1982 on the *Singing News* radio airplay chart.

Vocally, I didn't think it was the best recording. We had the tempo too fast or something; it just didn't have that special feel to it. It wasn't a perfect recording, but it sure put us on the map. It really was the story that sold the song. After all these years traveling and singing, "Antioch Church Choir" is still our most requested signature song.

I need to mention our steel guitar player Ron Wells, too. When we released "Antioch Church Choir," Ron was on the phone all the time calling radio stations to encourage the DJs to play it. He deserves a lot of the credit for the success of that song.

Like I said, I don't write very many songs, and most of my songs were only recorded by the Dixie Melody Boys. A few have been recorded by other groups, though.

We were in Tupelo, Mississippi one night at the ball field and the Rex Nelon Singers were with us. I came across the ball field on the way to the stadium and he was singing a song that I had no idea he even knew I wrote. It was called "Get Ready Brother."

No matter how good a group might be in terms of singing talent, they just can't survive without good songs. My good friend JD Sumner was a great songwriter. He told me about a young guy who came up to him at one of the early quartet conventions trying to pitch him a song. He told him, "Friend, I've written over 300 songs. If I'm going to record one, it's going to be one of mine."

He said that young man he turned down was Bill Gaither. JD did advise Bill to start a group, so he'd have an outlet for his songwriting. That seems to have worked out okay for him. JD later said if he had any idea Bill was going to be that successful, he would have been a lot nicer to him the first time they met!

You know, another successful songwriter in the industry is Mark Lowry who wrote the modern Christmas song "Mary Did You Know." It's on track to be a standard people will still be singing 100 years from now just like "Silent Night." Everyone has recorded it, and not just gospel groups.

It all starts with a song.

1975 album that included the first Dixie Melody Boys recording of "When I Cross To The Other Side Of Jordan"

1982 album that included the number one song "Antioch Church Choir"

(left to right) Ed Harper, Ed O'Neal, and Herman Harper
It was Herman Harper who suggested the Dixie Melody Boys record "Antioch Church Choir."

Chapter Seven: The DMB Band

By the time the mid-1980s rolled around, I began to wonder why more young people didn't come see us at our concerts. Believe it or not, I was young at one time myself and I loved it. I thought maybe it was the style of our music that needed to change and that instruments like drums and lead guitar in a country style might draw a young crowd.

Even before we made a deliberate shift in style, I noticed young people seemed to like some of the songs we were doing like "They're Holding Up the Ladder" that was written by the Easter Brothers. If you do that song with a good band, you'll see a reaction. "Step into the Water" is another one that had a country feel they really seemed to enjoy.

We recorded a couple of albums in 1983 and 1984 still billed as the Dixie Melody Boys, but in more of a country style. One song people remember from that period is "Good Ole Boys."

I saw a video someone had put together not long ago with the General Lee car from the *Dukes Of Hazzard* television show, but they were using our song rather than the original TV show theme recorded by Waylon Jennings.

When I first hired Frank Sutton, it was to play bass guitar. After our baritone left suddenly, I moved Frank to singing baritone. Later when our tenor singer left, I shifted Frank to tenor. That's when my son Allen started singing baritone.

My son Allen is a real singer's singer. He has one of the most fantastic voices. When we made the shift to this country or progressive style, Allen was our baritone. He had a lot of feature solos as well. We also had Kent Humphrey on lead. That combination of Frank, Kent, and Allen had what I called a magic sound.

Of course, I still sang bass, but in that style, you didn't hear much of me. The bass singer was usually buried in the mix. It wasn't meant to sound like a traditional Southern Gospel quartet.

The first album where the group name on the album cover changed to DMB Band was titled *Streetwise* (1985). One of the more progressive songs on that album was one Mike Payne wrote called "Gonna Make A Comeback." Mike had recorded some pretty heavy stuff himself, so I asked him why he didn't cut "Gonna Make A Comeback."

He said, "Are you kidding me?"

It really sounded a lot like some of the music the country group Alabama was recording in those years. When we were in the studio working on that song, our producer Wayne Hilton looked at me and said, "That'll keep you off of Bonifay."

Bonifay was a big concert event in Florida every year. Wayne Hilton was right. I didn't lose my fans, but I lost some of the concert promoters who had been faithfully booking the Dixie Melody Boys in the past. They were just afraid of promoting what we were trying to do alongside the traditional groups they were used to bringing in.

We did one more album billed as DMB Band that was titled *Run, Brother Run* (1986), but the label didn't push it. A popular contemporary Christian singer named Don Francisco ("He's Alive") was on the same label, Greentree Records, which was a part of the Benson music company. Greentree was pouring most of their resources into promoting Don Francisco at that time, and we were neglected.

One of my favorite promoters was up in Pennsylvania. He called and told me he would not be able to use us anymore. That night before I talked to him, we had been on stage with Squire Parsons and the Florida Boys and the people just ate it up. The fans loved it, but it was hard to book the same concert events I'd been used to getting with the promoters.

We did pick up a few new dates on contemporary festivals. I don't know how many thousand people we sang for in Front Royal, Virginia. It was on a mountainside just covered with people. The ones in the back were so far from the stage they almost looked like ants. The PA system they had there was so big they called it the "Million Dollar Sound System."

Another event we worked like that was held in Rapid City, South Dakota. Afterward, we drove the bus out to see Mount Rushmore which wasn't too far away.

At the time we were also doing a lot of work for *The PTL Club*. Jim Bakker liked us, and we were close by. He could call the night before and I could be in Charlotte the next morning taping a television show with him. There were many places on that campus you could sing, and they always had a crowd there. We did that quite a bit, and that helped sustain us for a while.

George Younce and Glen Payne were always my friends, but they didn't care much for what I was trying to do. Claude Hopper didn't like it much either. I didn't lose any of them as friends, understand, and I don't blame anyone but myself for it not working out. I was the one who wanted to do it, and I chose the songs.

In the years since, many people have said we were just about ten years ahead of our time. Karen Peck was a big fan, and when she started her own group, you may remember that she had a full band of musicians. Even now, she still records a lot of songs with a country feel. Sheri Easter was one of our devoted fans, too. She was still Sheri Lewis at the time. I'll tell you a funny story about Sheri and her love for the DMB Band later in this book.

We gave the DMB Band our best shot, but after a few years, I realized I just couldn't go any further with it. I took it off the road in August of 1987.

I called Paul Heil who had one of Southern Gospel music's top radio shows at the time; he still does, as a matter of fact. It's called *The Gospel Greats*. I said, "Paul, I've took the band off the road, and I've decided to get me a traditional quartet back. If you can, please make an announcement on your next radio broadcast to let all the people know."

Glen Payne was in Rockwell, Texas when he heard Paul Heil mention that on the air. Glen got on the phone and called me that same day. The first words he said when I picked up were, "Praise God!"

But you know, everything comes around in due time. Back a few years ago, I wanted to do something a little different for my homecoming concert. I asked McCray Dove if he had any ideas, and he said, "Why don't you get the old DMB Band back?"

I said, "Wow, it's been more than 25 years and I don't even know how to get in touch with them."

McCray said, "If I contact them and get them squared away, will you put them on the program?"

Well, he got them together and they agreed to come. Along with my son Allen, Frank Sutton, and Kent Humphrey singing, they had Olan Witt on drums, Craig Ham on lead guitar, and Jerry Kelso playing piano.

I'm telling you the truth, when they stepped on the stage, and started the first song, it sounded like they'd never quit. We didn't know if anyone remembered DMB Band or if they did whether they'd even care, but a lot of fans and friends showed up.

After that they decided to start singing again and they're still out there doing it today. They call themselves Jackson Heights now, and they still have that magic sound I talked about before. They are very talented. They've put together a top-notch production with colored lights synced up to the music to enhance each song.

Of course, the way they work now, they don't have to depend on it for an income like we did in the DMB Band days. They sing about ten dates in the spring and ten in the fall with a few in between during the summer. Allen has a great job and Olan has a bus leasing company. A couple of the other members have changed since they rebranded as Jackson Heights.

You know, I mentioned before that the DMB Band was ten years ahead of our time. There was a group doing a similar style that followed us around to concerts back then during our DMB Band years. They were called MidSouth and they thought we were bigger than Pepsi-Cola.

After I took the DMB Band off the road, our lead singer Kent Humphrey joined MidSouth and was still with them during the 1990s when they had a big song called "Without You (I Haven't Got a Prayer)." It won a Dove Award in 1996, and they were very well received and respected at that time.

There definitely was a real market emerging for the Christian Country music that my son Allen and I were trying to create with the DMB Band in the 1980s. Maybe you could call us pioneers.

We just got there a little too early to be successful with it.

The Dixie Melody Boys' 1983 album More Than Just Good Ole Boys *set the stage for the DMB Band*

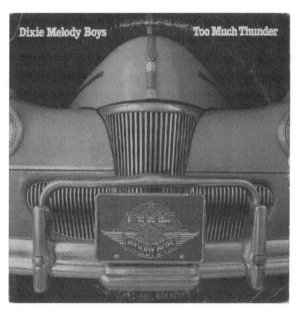

This 1984 cover still used the Dixie Melody Boys brand, but the group was making a deliberate shift to what would become the DMB Band by this point.

The first album branded DMB Band was titled Streetwise *and released in 1985*

The second and final DMB Band album titled Run Little Brother *was released in 1986*

Jackson Heights includes several former DMB Band members (left to right) Frank Sutton, Danny Samples, Kent Humphrey, Jeremy Edwards, Allen O'Neal, Olan Witt

Chapter Eight: Return to Traditional Quartet

After I made the decision to pull the band off the road and reorganize a traditional quartet, I had to hire new singers. My daughter-in-law Teresa (Allen's wife) was my secretary when the DMB Band was still up and running. She said a fellow had called just a few weeks before and said he'd be interested in a job if I ever needed another singer.

I said, "Who was it?"

She said, "I don't know, but I think I put his name and number under that typewriter."

She found the number and gave it to me with his name, McCray Dove, and I called him. He wasn't at home, but his mother said she'd give him the information and make sure he called me back. He called me that afternoon right away.

I said, "McCray, can you come up and see how we sound together?"

He said, "I sure can. When do you want to do it?"

I said, "Can you come in the morning?"

He said, "Yes, I can."

This short little skinny fellow showed up to try out the next day. He looked like a little knot and was just seventeen years old. His hair was so long in the back that he could have pulled it around to the front and worn it like a necklace.

Now, I don't like to do tryouts with music. I want to hear the voice. It makes it harder on the singer, but they're really trying their best when there are no instruments.

I said, "McCray, just pick a song and sing it for me."

He chose the song "There's Power in Prayer." I'm serious when I tell you that when he got through singing, the water was flowing out of my eyes and dripping off of my chin. I knew then that McCray was my man. He's probably not the best singer that ever lived, but I've never known a greater communicator than McCray Dove.

I told him he could have the job, but I said first he had to get rid of that hair. Would you believe he took me literally?

The next time he showed up, he had almost all of it buzzed off. He was quite a sight to see. I took him to my barber, but there was very little he could do to improve it before we went out for our first dates.

Along with McCray, I hired Larry DeLawder to play harmonica. Larry was such a talented guy who could play multiple instruments. I had first considered Larry as a piano player, but then I hired David Ledford to free up Larry to be more of a utility musician. We called David Ledford "Bobby." Keep reading and you'll find out in a minute why we didn't call him David.

Completing the group was Larry's brother David DeLawder singing baritone and David Walker on tenor. Now I haven't mentioned this yet, but McCray's first name also happens to be David. That's right. Aside from Larry DeLawder, every young man I had just hired was named David.

I told them we had to decide on something different for some of them so as not to confuse the fans, you know. McCray's full name is David McCray Dove, but he had gone by McCray his whole life, so that was easily settled. The piano player said his middle name was Robert, but we could call him Bobby. We decided to shorten one of the others to "Dave," and that's how I introduced them on stage.

We were still green at that point and getting used to each other, but we recorded a quick album just so we would have something to sell at our first concerts. McCray had only been with us about a week when we made that recording.

The first weekend we went out and worked three dates in Virginia (Front Royal, Fairfield, and Watermelon Park). Our last concert before we came back home was at the Joyful Noise supper club in East Point, Georgia which is just southwest of Atlanta.

That was how the group came to be put together in the fall of 1987. Within a few months, though, David Walker and David DeLawder were gone. At that point I hired Derrick Boyd to sing tenor and Nathan Widener to sing baritone. That was a good quartet, and the first one that I took into the studio to do a professional quality album.

I called Eddie Crook who was one of the top producers at the time, and said, "Do you have a quartet on your label?"

Eddie said, "No, I don't."

I said, "Well, would you like to have one?"

Eddie said, "Why don't you drop by here when you're coming through and we'll talk about it."

I did, and that was the beginning of an 11-year partnership.

We released an album titled *Back Home* on Eddie's Harvest Records label in 1988. With the move from the DMB Band back to a traditional quartet and all the singers changing, we were considered new at that point. Eddie said he couldn't put me on his main label (Morningstar Records) immediately, so we did that first album on Harvest, which he used for his up-and-coming artists.

Every year since 1970, *Singing News* magazine has presented what they call the Fan Awards. Subscribers to the magazine vote for their favorites in a bunch of different categories. For 1988, *Singing News* added a few new categories to the Fan Awards including one called Favorite Horizon Group. The Dixie Melody Boys were included in the list of nominees and went on to win it that year!

That may seem a bit odd for a group as old as mine to win an award called "Horizon" that would usually be reserved for brand new groups, but we really were brand new at the time. The Dixie Melody Boys name had been around, of course, but it had not been used while I had the DMB Band. As far as the singers and musicians were concerned, everyone other than me was brand new to the industry at that time

It meant a lot to them and to me for us to be recognized. I was grateful that Maurice Templeton who was the publisher at *Singing News* at the time allowed us to be considered for that category. It helped get us on the forefront in people's minds again.

Maurice Templeton was always a good friend to me and the Dixie Melody Boys. I may say this several times before I finish this book, but it's worth repeating. You just can't do this thing without some help. Maurice helped us that time and I sure appreciated it!

The following year, in 1989, Eddie Crook moved us up to his main label called Morningstar Records. The album that we recorded and released that year was titled *Ridin' High*.

The same line-up of Derrick, McCray, Nathan, and me had been together for a couple of years at that point and I was very happy with the way that record turned out. I really enjoyed that entire 10-11 years when we were recording with Eddie Crook.

I told Eddie when I went to record for his label that I'm the world's worst self-promoter. I can sing and present a quality program, but I just never have felt right constantly pushing myself on people. I told Eddie, "I want you to do it."

I can't brag on myself, and when other people do that too much, it tends to turn me off. It is one thing to be confident in what I can do, but I never want to come across as being too cocky.

In fact, it was Eddie Crook who encouraged me to start billing the group as Ed O'Neal & the Dixie Melody Boys rather than just using the group name. Eddie said, "No matter who comes and goes at the other positions, you're going to be the constant one that fans will associate with the group."

Eddie Crook was one of the best in the business and treated us right. Most record labels have a clause in their contract guaranteeing they'll get back their production costs off the top. Eddie always sold us our product for the cost of manufacture right away. I told an executive from another label who was trying to get us to record with them about this one time, and he couldn't believe it. We sold a lot of product when we were with him. I really had no reason to quit when I parted ways with Eddie Crook. I wasn't upset or anything. I had just decided at that point that I wanted to do my own thing. Our last album with Eddie Crook was titled *Live in Music City*. It came out in 1998.

I've always tried to be nice to people. One thing I've done over the years in this business is I've made friends, and I've kept friends.

When one of my boys decides to quit, I don't try to talk them into staying. Sometimes I'm asked if I thought a particular singer might have stayed if I offered them more money. He might for a while, but when he gets to that point, he sees something else out there that he wants. If I try to talk him into staying by offering more money, I can become the enemy that's standing in the way of his dream. I let them go follow their dream so we can stay friends.

There are few people in the business that I've been crossways with. I don't know of any really. Of course, sometimes I think some are going about it the wrong way, but it's not my place to tell them. If they call and ask, of course, then I'll give them some advice.

McCray Dove was my lead singer from the day he first showed up with long hair to audition in 1987 until he started the Dove Brothers some ten or eleven years later. He was a showman and the people really loved him. The best years I ever had financially were when he was with me.

Except for some dates that we did with the Cathedrals, the Kingsmen, and the Happy Goodman Family, promoters put us on as the closing group at almost every concert. We weren't always booked as the headliner, but they knew that crowd was going to come up when McCray got through doing his thing. As I said, McCray was such a good communicator. In fact, he can get to a crowd without jumping around.

He is a student of the history of the music, too. Any time he was with me and we were on a program with another group, you could find him with somebody like Les Beasley or JD Sumner or Claude Hopper just soaking up everything they had to say.

History repeated itself for McCray, too. Just like we had done with the Dixie Melody Boys after his first year with me, McCray and his Dove Brothers won the Favorite Horizon Group category for the *Singing News* Fan Awards after their first full year out there in 1999. I was so proud of all he was able to do and cheered him on after he moved on. McCray was with me a long time and remains one of my dearest friends.

It really was unusual anyway for me to keep the same singer for more than ten years. As a matter of fact, I hold the record among group owners for having more turnover than anyone else in this industry, but I've kept them as friends.

Now let me tell you something about singing gospel music. Most of us never get rich. You might be comfortable at times, but you won't get rich.

The most money I ever made was not singing, but related to singing, and that was when I would sell a bus or something. You've got to be tight, too. That's the reason I bought a van a few years ago. The last time I had a bus, I spent $70,000 in one year just for fuel! Whether you buy a new bus or a used bus, you're going to have a breakdown.

The way we were going back then, though, with four singers, a driver, and at least a couple of musicians, we couldn't have done it without a bus. We traveled to almost every state in the United States and got into Canada from time to time as well. I had a nice shower on the last bus I had, and that really makes a difference, too.

I think I've had 10 or 11 buses over the years. Times have certainly changed. When I bought my first bus, I could buy diesel fuel for 29.9 cents per gallon. I could start with $100 in my pocket and go all weekend, maybe up to Delaware or Maryland, and I'd still have change when I got back home.

The most depressed I ever was about a bus breaking down happened in San Antonio, Texas. I didn't think we'd ever get there. Eric Ollis was with me at the time and he did a lot of the driving at night. I was in there talking with the promoter after the concert and thanking him while Eric was getting the bus ready to go. He came in and said, "I think we have a problem."

I said, "What's that?"

He said, "We've got water in the oil."

I said, "I'll be out there in a minute."

When we pulled the stick out, it measured way too high which confirmed we had water in the oil. I called a diesel service company to pull it over to a shop. The next morning, I went over to check on it and couldn't find anyone there who could speak English, so I decided to have it brought back to Atlanta. I paid a fortune just for that.

Then the trouble started. They rebuilt the engine four times. Two times I couldn't even get it home before it quit again. I finally had to get my lawyer involved to get them to make it right.

That sort of thing combined with the high cost of diesel fuel are the two main reasons my boys travel in a Sprinter van now. I bought it brand new in 2008, and it has close to 600,000 miles on it now. We can pull into a campground and plug in to their electrical supply to operate our air conditioning and TV. Of course, we will have to replace a part now and then, but that's nothing like a bus repair.

A bus can break you. Even a new bus is going to give you a problem sooner or later. That convenience is nice, but there are just so many things that can go wrong.

Claude Hopper had bought a brand new one, and we were with them at Twitty City. As we were leaving, I said, "Well, bud, I hope you get out of town without breaking down in your new bus."

They all laughed.

About two o'clock in the morning, Michael Hopper called me. He said, "Man, don't wish us luck no more."

I said, "Why?"

He said, "Our transmission just went out on our brand-new bus!"

Well, I could talk about buses stranding us and other groups some more, but that's enough about buses. Now, I'm going to tell you how I've seen music change over the years.

Looking back, I guess I've recorded music on almost every type of format. I came along a little too late to record any 78s, but we did make an acetate recording at someone's house with the O'Neal Trio when I was a kid singing tenor. Of course, I've been on music that was released on LP albums at 33 1/3 rpm, singles at 45 rpm, 8-tracks, cassettes, and CDs. When they told me cassettes were coming on and 8-tracks were on the way out, I didn't believe them. I had a warehouse full of them for a while. I finally got rid of them by offering them for $1 each.

Along with CDs in recent years, we've also offered some of our music through digital MP3 downloads and streaming. Now LP albums are making a comeback, but I don't think I want to start lugging those things around again.

I've attended most of the National Quartet Conventions since going to Memphis all those years ago in 1970. We've made many fun memories there including some you'll find in another chapter of this book. This memory is more touching than funny, though, so I thought it would be appropriate to share it here.

The last time my buddy Jim Hamill was able to attend NQC before he passed away in 2007, he and I shared the stage as part of a one-time "All Star Quartet." *Singing News* magazine assembled the group to sing during their Fan Awards. Joining Jim and I were Archie Watkins of the Inspirations singing tenor, Glen Allred of the Florida Boys singing baritone, and my old record producer Eddie Crook playing the piano. That was such a special moment to me.

In 2006, I reached the biblical age of fourscore and ten (70). Around this time people began to notice the Dixie Melody Boys were singing a mellower style of music than we had in the past. This was not a coincidence. I needed to slow down a little bit. Seeing my boys climbing speakers and jumping off a tall stage into the crowd had been a thrilling rush 20 years earlier. Now it just caused me to have a panic attack.

Thankfully, the folks continued to welcome our more sedate style of singing. Fast forward another 14 years to 2020, and you can say I've certainly seen a lot of things come and go. My memory is one of them. I can't recall every detail like I could in the past, but I can still tell a funny story. We have had some great times out on the road.

Not long ago, my publicist Deana Surles Warren called me up and said the Gaither tour was coming to New Bern, North Carolina. She said if I wanted to go, she'd get me some seats in the artist circle. I said sure. It's just 30 miles or so from my house.

She called back and said if I was coming, Bill wanted me to come early and eat with him. I did, and we had a good time of fellowship together.

During the latter part of the program, that Crabb boy (Adam) came down and got me by the arm. He said, "Bill wants you up on the stage."

I said, "Man, I can't get up them steps."

He said, "Oh yeah, you can get up the steps."

I said, "Man, I'm telling you, I can't."

About then, here came Bill Gaither's backup bass singer Gene McDonald down the steps, and the two of them helped me get up on to the stage. I laughed and said, "Well, I've made it now. I've finally sung with the Gaither Vocal Band."

Someone asked me recently whose voice is the finest I've ever heard in my career, not just limited to the Dixie Melody Boys, but out of all the singers I'd ever heard. From the old days, the best tenor voice I can remember was Jim Murray who sang with the Imperials.

In more recent years, there's very few who can hold a candle to David Phelps who sang two tenures with the Gaither Vocal Band and now does solo concerts. He's just something you can't hardly believe you're hearing. He's awesome. We did a concert with him a few years ago, and he and I met out in the hall before it started. He said, "Mr. O'Neal"

I said, "Please, call me Ed."

He said, "Would you take a picture with me?"

I said, "I was just about to ask you the same thing!"

People who live near me might know what I did in a general sense, but they don't really know what I did. They just knew I'd be gone most every Thursday through Sunday and that I'd be back usually on Monday.

My health has slowed me down in the past few years. I hurt my right vertebrae on a golf cart when a guy driving it took off before I had got completely on it. I dealt with that for a year before I found somebody that could take care of it. I finally found one that was supposed to be the best in Raleigh. I went to him with an MRI and he said he thought he could fix it. You could see on the MRI where the fifth vertebra was pinching a nerve. That doctor said he'd just have to go in and make some room for it, and he did.

Then, last year, when the doctor put that pacemaker in, he said, "Don't be swinging no golf club until the first of March. You've got two wires stuck in your heart. You don't want to pull them out."

That was in September of 2019. I don't know if I could keep up with them, though. I'm too short-winded. That pacemaker will keep my heart rate from dropping below 70 beats per minute, but it's not going to keep it from going up too high.

It's a different life when you're by yourself. If I need anything from upstairs at my house now, Rayburn Lane comes by almost every morning, and I'll ask him to go up and get it. At my age, every day it seems like there's some new pain I didn't have the day before.

But I'm still going.

Bobby Ledford and McCray Dove at Watermelon Park in Virginia the first weekend the Dixie Melody Boys returned to a traditional quartet format

*1990 Dixie Melody Boys
(left to right) McCray Dove, Nathan Widener, Ed O'Neal, Steve Wood, Derrick Boyd, Larry DeLawder*

*1993 Dixie Melody Boys
(left to right) Derrick Boyd, McCray Dove, Rodney Griffin, Ed O'Neal*

*1993 Dixie Melody Boys
(left to right) McCray Dove, Eric Ollis, Ed O'Neal, Larry DeLawder, Derrick Boyd, Rodney Griffin*

The Dixie Melody Boys put a lot of miles on this bus they called "Big Red."

*1997 Dixie Melody Boys
(left to right) McCray Dove, Harold Reed, Ed O'Neal, Craig Singletary, Eric Ollis*

2003 Dixie Melody Boys
(left to right) Eric Ollis, Derrick Selph, Harold Reed, Ed O'Neal, Devin McGlamery

2005 Dixie Melody Boys
(left to right) Dustin Sweatman, Andrew King, Ed O'Neal, Dan Keeton

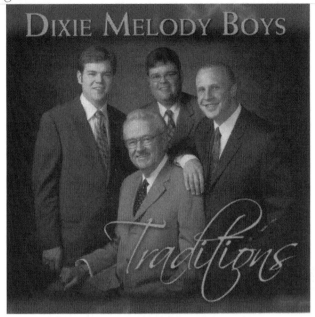

2006 Dixie Melody Boys
(left to right) Andrew King, Ed O'Neal, Dan Keeton, Bryan Walker

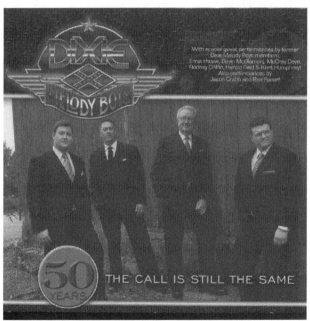

2011 Dixie Melody Boys
(left to right) Donald Morris, Matt Felts, Ed O'Neal, Steven Cooper

2013 Dixie Melody Boys
(left to right) Andrew Dishman, Ed O'Neal, Matt Felts, Josh Garner

2015 Dixie Melody Boys
(left to right) Josh Garner, Doug Pittman, Aaron Dishman, Ed O'Neal

Ed O'Neal bought this bus from McCray Dove and had it painted gold.

Chapter Nine: Ed O'Neal University

Like I mentioned in the previous chapter, I guess I've had more turnover of members than any other group owner in the business.

I'd have to look at a list just to try to remember all of them. Many of them went on to sing full-time with other groups. I watched the groups as they came across the stage one year at the National Quartet Convention. Every 15 to 20 minutes, another group would go on, and that night I had a former member in almost every group that sang!

One thing I have never done is try to keep a singer once they say they're thinking about moving on. Offering another $50 ain't going to keep them. I'd rather have a friend out there than an enemy and I just never let it bother me when one of them would leave. I might have been upset for a minute when one might leave without much of a notice, but I never let that last. I've always believed that once they've decided to go, the best thing for me to do is let them go. That way, we can stay friends.

A curious thing I realized a few years after my wife passed away was that I really have very few friends from the town where I live. There are a few old cutthroats here that I play golf with, but I was always gone all those years. I've been blessed with MANY friends, understand, but most of the people I'd call my true friends are people I've know that also sang gospel music. They live all over and many of them are former employees of mine.

In this chapter I'm just going to mention some former members of the Dixie Melody Boys who are now collectively called the alumni of Ed O'Neal University. I must start with Rodney Griffin, because it was Rodney who came up with the idea for EOU in the first place. After that, the names are in no specific order.

Rodney Griffin
Rodney Griffin was my baritone singer from 1992 to 1993 before he took Mark Trammell's place with Greater Vision. He's a special guy.

He got his start with the Brashear Family. He'd been to hear them sing. Rodney got to talking with them after the concert and said his dream was to sing full-time. They said, "Well, buddy, get on our bus and we'll show you full-time."

I don't think he made much money with them, but he did get an idea of what "full-time" was like. He clearly had a love for it because that's all he's ever done since that time. When he came to join the Dixie Melody Boys, he joked that it felt like he was on vacation.

Some years later we were together for some function and Rodney made the comment that he'd learned more being on my bus for a few years than he'd learned in four years of college. From that joke Rodney made, one thing led to another and the whole concept of Ed O'Neal University (EOU) got started. We had a special shirt made for the former members to wear. I've still got some of them.

Of course, Rodney has written a lot of great songs over the years. I kind of teased him recently and asked him why he didn't write songs like that when he was with me. Now, he had started writing some back then. In fact, I had published one of his songs, but it was before he started churning out all those hits.

Years later I went to visit Rodney. He'd been after me to come see him. I got the address and drove out there, but all I could see was this big mansion on a hill. I called him again and said, "Rodney, give me your address again, I think I wrote it down wrong."

He said, "Are you in your red pickup? I think you just passed me."

I said, "Yeah."

He said, "Look up on the hill."

Writing songs appears to have paid off for Rodney.

When I got hurt and Greater Vision was nearby in Myrtle Beach, South Carolina for the big annual Singing in The Sun event, they called and asked if they could come see me. The whole group came by. I was sick and laid out there.

Rodney told me later that when they went back to their bus to leave, Gerald Wolfe said he didn't think I was going to make it. Rodney came back a second time when he was going to Myrtle Beach on vacation. He said he wanted to take a picture of me and send it to Gerald!

I guess of all the people I've known in this business over the years, Rodney probably calls me more than anyone else. I talked to him just a few days before I started working on this book. I told him I was going to need his help remembering some of the things that needed to be included.

I really want the book to be entertaining, and I guess if you've read this far, maybe it is.

Tony Brown
We must go back the very beginning for Tony Brown. He was with the Dixie Melody Boys when I first joined, and just a kid as I explained in a previous chapter. Even though I didn't own the group at the time, I still count him as one of the first graduates of EOU. Tony went on to play for the Stamps and

the Oak Ridge Boys. He was in a trio with Reba Rambo and Greg Gordon called Charity's Children as well.

Tony should be a wealthy man now. He became head of MCA Records for several years, and after he left there, he started his own production company. He's responsible for George Strait's albums and Reba McEntire's and countless other major names in the Country field.

Jamie Bramlett

Jamie Bramlett sang and drove the bus for us for a while. He had been with Rodney Griffin before in The Brashears. We were needing someone to drive and Rodney recommended Jamie. I told Rodney to call him, and he came.

Jamie saw me at convention one night not too long after we'd made those EOU shirts. He came up and said, "I never did get one of them shirts."

I said, "You didn't graduate."

We had a good laugh about that. Jamie wasn't really a solo singer, but he was a very good baritone singer. He had the kind of tone that would blend with just about anybody and he could carry the part.

Ernie Haase

Everyone knows Ernie Haase from his time singing tenor with the Cathedrals, the Old Friends Quartet, and now his own group Signature Sound. Very few remember that he sang with the Dixie Melody Boys because he was only with us a short time.

We were in the process of transitioning to the DMB Band when Ernie joined the group. Now, Ernie Haase is obviously one of the most accomplished and successful tenor singers in the business, but his tone just didn't match that Country sound we were trying to create with the band. His time with the Dixie Melody Boys was too sudden and short.

He went on to sing with Squire Parsons for a while and then ended up with a little group in Stow, Ohio you might have heard of called the Cathedrals. He married the boss' daughter, too.

Ernie was only in the Dixie Melody Boys for a month and a half or so, but we're still friends. I saw him when Signature Sound was just getting hot, and he asked me to come over and meet his group. He took me over and told them who I was. They all jumped up and one of them said, "Ed O'Neal, can you really walk on water?"

Ernie Haase is a fine human being; I can tell you that. We're still good buddies. I'm happy to see him having success.

Derrick Boyd
Derrick Boyd joined the Dixie Melody Boys after David Walker had been with us just a short time. A few years ago, he returned and started singing with us again. Derrick has a different way of singing than most tenors.

I don't travel with the group now, but I went to see them a few nights ago when they were about an hour away from the house. I was amazed at his singing. He's been a good employee.

Earl Roberts

When I was looking for a lead singer just last year, Earl Roberts brought a guy to meet me. Earl himself wasn't looking for a job, but when he spoke, I asked if he sang. He replied that he did, and after listening to him, I realized he can sing lower than I ever could.

The guys had traveled as a trio for a while after I came off the road, but Earl is singing bass with them now. He is really what we needed to give the fans that quartet sound that they expect from the Dixie Melody Boys. We had Will Lane singing bass for a short time before he moved on to the LeFevre Quartet. Earl stepped right in after Will left and he's done a great job for us.

Harold Reed

One of the finest tenors I ever had in the Dixie Melody Boys was Harold Reed. He traveled with us for eleven years and was a great employee as well as a great person. He was happy to sing anything I ever asked him to sing.

Harold joined us while McCray was still the lead singer and those two made a good pair with the way they'd work off of each other. Harold was in the group from 1993 to 2004 and he's still a good singer. After singing with us, he went with the Florida Boys and later the Kingsmen.

Jamie Caldwell

Jamie Caldwell followed McCray Dove in 1997 and was with us until 2000. We taped "Antioch Church Choir" for a Gaither video with Jamie and that's my all-time favorite cut of that song. In fact, I looked over at Gloria Gaither when he was singing it, and she was crying. She said she hadn't heard the song before and asked me where I found it.

Jamie has filled in for us off and on in the past few years when we needed a lead singer. Jamie is a great preacher and has a church in Georgia. He's been so good to fly in anywhere I need him.

I'd say Jamie Caldwell is probably the best singer I've ever had in the group in terms of his vocal technique.

Devin McGlamery

I've started a lot of kids off when they were just teenagers, and Devin McGlamery was one of those. He followed Jamie Caldwell in the early 2000s and was with me for about four years. The first time I took Devin to the National Quartet Convention, his mom had bought him a bunch of clothes. He dressed three times before we sang!

Devin was from Valdosta, Georgia, but while he was with the Dixie Melody Boys he lived near my home in Kinston, North Carolina. After singing with the Dixie Melody Boys, Devin went on to sing with Karen Peck & New River.

Working with Karen about wore him out, because he was still living in Kinston and meeting them wherever they were going each weekend. Devin landed with Ernie Haase & Signature Sound after that and they've done well together.

Bryan Walker

Bryan Walker has a unique voice and he's a good singer. He sang lead and baritone for a about a year or so. He also competed on *American Idol*.

Bryan went to the Perrys and after that, he got out of the singing business for a while. He's back singing again with Legacy Five now. I'm glad people are getting the chance to hear him again.

Derrick Selph

A year or two before Devin McGlamery joined the group, Derrick Selph came to the Dixie Melody Boys to sing baritone. After Devin joined us, the two of them rented a place together near me in Kinston. After spending about five years with us, Derrick moved on to join Brian Free & Assurance in 2003.

That lasted ten years with one break, I think, and then he moved back to my area. Derrick wasn't from here originally, but he married a girl from here and we go to the same church now. I was raised as a Baptist, but my kids go to the Church of God, so that's where I go now.

Derrick still uses his talent for singing at church there.

Aaron Dishman

I love this kid. He played piano and sang baritone for the Dixie Melody Boys for about three years and was one I really hated to see go. After the Dixie Melody Boys, he was with Triumphant for a while.

He's working for UPS now in Mobile, Alabama, but still gets out and sings with his wife on the weekends. Aaron calls me ever so often to catch up and keeps me in the loop on what he's doing. He's a good guy.

Josh Garner
Most of the singers I've had in the Dixie Melody Boys have been young guys starting out, but Josh Garner was already well-known for his time in the Florida Boys long before he came to sing for me. When the Florida Boys retired, he did solo work for a while, and then he was in Freedom Quartet with John Rulapaugh.

When I needed a lead singer in 2013, he called one day. He said, "If I can help you by filling in, let me know."

He worked out real good. He's a great singer. After some time, he asked me one day, "Why don't you just keep me and quit looking?"

I agreed and he stayed with us for five years or maybe a little more. He didn't relocate close by. I don't think I could have done what he did traveling back and forth all those miles, but I was grateful that he did.

Herman Harper
I've said before that you can't make it in the business with a lot of help. Herman Harper never sang with the Dixie Melody

Boys, but he was critical to us being able to operate. Herman was my booking agent when we were getting started, and he kept that date book full...Thursday, Friday, Saturday, and Sunday...week in and week out.

Herman wouldn't represent more than 13 groups at any given time. That was his limit. I had to wait a full year to finally be added to his roster. Someone else had to leave before he'd add me.

When he was representing us, I could look at our date book on December 31, and we wouldn't have an open date until after June. I hardly ever had to pick up the phone to try to schedule a date myself.

Dustin Sweatman
We got a great singer and piano player in Dustin Sweatman when he came to us in 2003. He sang baritone and lead as well as playing piano. One of the best old-time sounding line-ups we had was when he was with me. We did an appearance on the Grand Ole Gospel Reunion that's on YouTube if you want to look it up. That appeals to the older fans...piano and four singers.

Dustin is the music director in Georgia at the church where Jamie Caldwell preaches now.

Matt Felts
Matt Felts joined us in 2010 to sing tenor. Matt is a fine singer, but I tell you what his real talent is: marketing. He helped

design those Ed O'Neal University shirts and kept us in the press while he was with us.

Matt travels with Carman now and works as his manager. I know Carman from back in the days when we were both on PTL with Jim and Tammy Faye Bakker. Sometimes when Matt calls me now, I get to touch base with Carman again and laugh about some of the things we did all those years ago.

Steven Cooper
Steven Cooper worked with me for a while singing baritone and driving the bus. He was a good singer for us, and a smooth driver, too. That's what you need if you're in a gospel group.

He's driving for the Oak Ridge Boys now. Anytime I talk to Steven on the phone and Duane Allen realizes he's talking to me, he'll say, "Let me talk to Ed for a minute."

Duane is a real student of gospel music history. He knows how to pick a great song, too. I've known him for a long time. Steven says they're just a bunch of old men who go out and sing and then each one does his own thing on the bus.

Eric Ollis
My piano player for about twelve years was Eric Ollis. Eric would get excited at the piano sometimes. He'd stand up and take his coat off and sling it out into the crowd.

After he was with us, Eric went on to play for the Whisnants for several years. I was walking by their booth at the next

National Quartet Convention after he went with them when Susan Whisnant stopped me and said, "Ed, I hope it didn't upset you that Eric left you and came to work with us."

I said, "Oh no, it didn't. As a matter of fact, I ought to buy you a steak."

She said, "What do I need to know?"

We had a good laugh about that.

Eric's boy now is just like his daddy. He calls me sometimes as often as three times a week. When I answer the phone, he always starts the conversation with, "Hello, Mr. Ed" and then after we talk a while he'll say, "I love you Mr. Ed. I'll talk to you later."

Rayburn Lane
Rayburn Lane is probably the best friend I've ever had in this world. His mother started bringing him to see us when he was just a boy. He was 11 or 12 years old and used to tell us we all looked like a bunch of sissies in our fancy suits. We'd laugh at him. He'd say a man was supposed to wear a black suit, white socks, black shoes, etc.

Rayburn's mother brought him all the way to West Virginia to see us one time for his birthday. That's how much he loved it.

After he got out of high school, he started riding with us. He sat up front in the buddy seat when I was driving. This was around 1983 or 1984. After this went on for a couple of weeks, we were coming out of Fort Worth, Texas one morning and I'd been driving all night. I was tired. When Rayburn woke up and came up front, I said, "Rayburn, you're not as smart as I thought you was."

He asked me, "What do you mean?"

I said, "You've been sitting there for two weeks or more watching me drive this bus, tired as I am, and you haven't made a dime. If you'd get down here and drive some, I'd pay something for it."

Rayburn says now that what I paid him was a "little something." He says I left the "little" part out when I first offered him a job!

I tell him that no matter how little I paid him, I made even less.

I taught Rayburn to drive, and now he's been with me off and on for more than 30 years. He's been all over the world with me. We used to do a lot up in the eastern part of Canada.

Rayburn left us to drive for the Dove Brothers when they got started, because he and McCray were always good buddies, but eventually he came back to drive for me. He's been loyal. If you ever have anything bad to say about me, don't say it around him!

Pretty much his entire life, Rayburn's only jobs have been farming and driving a bus either for me or for McCray. I don't have a bus for him to drive now, so he just drives me around wherever I need to go in a car. He took me more than halfway across North Carolina more than one time just so I could do the interviews with the man who is helping me put this book together!

When I had my accident, my daughter Dara wouldn't let me stay at home. I had to stay at her house. I was there about four months flat on my back. I don't know if she talked to Rayburn or not, but when I came home, he was there. He's over at my house almost every morning to cook my breakfast and help me get the day started.

He says all those years ago, he never dreamed he'd be helping take care of me when I retired. He is a good guy. You just can't make it in this business without friends. Rayburn Lane is right there at the top of my list of friends. I couldn't ask for a better one.

A once in a lifetime photo of Rayburn Lane wearing a tuxedo with Joy and Ed O'Neal on the occasion of Ed's induction into the Southern Gospel Music Association's Hall of Fame in 2004

Another image of Ed O'Neal with Rayburn Lane wearing their tuxedos

Ed O'Neal and Rayburn Lane selling product and meeting fans

Ed Harper of the Harper Agency and Ed O'Neal on the golf course

Ed O'Neal, George Younce, Herman Harper's sister-in-law, and Ray Dean Reese at the 1982 Marvin Norcross Memorial Golf Classic tournament

Paul Downing and Ed O'Neal (in the center) at the 1985 Marvin Norcross Memorial Golf Classic tournament with two other men who attended that day

Ed O'Neal, Bob Brumley, unidentified lady (she worked at the golf course), and former LeFevres bass singer Jimmy Jones at the 1989 Marvin Norcross Memorial Golf Classic tournament

Chapter Ten: Joy O'Neal

You've already read about how Joy and I were married on July 4, 1956 after I set the date as a joke. I never would have had this career in music without her by my side supporting me.

I truly was blessed in life to have a wife who allowed me to follow my dream of singing. Instead of a normal work week with weekends off, I was usually out of town Thursday through Sunday, and sometimes longer than that if we were doing something like a west coast tour that might last three weeks.

Joy knew that I had been called to this ministry, and she was willing to make the sort of sacrifices that were required which included acting at times as both the mother and the father to our three children. When the family went on what we called a "vacation" during the summer months, it was usually paired with some event where I was singing.

She usually traveled with me and the group during the week of the National Quartet Convention. Back during the early 1970s, JD Sumner would invite Elvis Presley to come to the convention each year. I remember one year we went when our son Allen was about twelve years old, just bouncing off the walls, young and energetic. He did not miss anything that was going on either. He came running over to me all excited and said, "Elvis is here!"

Joy said, "Please son, go sit down. You're running all over this auditorium."

Allen said, "No, he's here! I saw him go in that back room!"

She didn't believe Allen, but sure enough, Elvis was there. He was introduced and came out. Of course, he wasn't there to perform. All he did was walk across the stage and wave at the people. The flashbulbs going off made it look like a war zone in there.

Now I should point out here that Joy had made a statement in the past several times that went something like this: "I like Elvis' singing, but I do not understand why these girls get excited and go to screaming and hollering when Elvis comes around. I don't understand that!"

Later in the day when there was a break in the program, a lot of people started gathering down around the stage door. They thought Elvis was going to come out that way. Joy went down there with them. I said, "Joy, he's not going to come out that way. There's too many people, and they'll take him out another way."

She didn't believe me, so she went down there with several hundred more people waiting for Elvis to come out. At the same time, my baritone singer and I were standing where we could see this crowd, but we were up at the side of the building.

There were two or three exits on the auditorium between us and the stage door where everyone had gathered. We were standing there watching and talking about how crazy those people were waiting on Elvis to come out.

While we stood there, I noticed that two guys came out of the exit behind us, looked both ways, and went back in. A few seconds later, here came Elvis out that door. He was in a black suit with one of those short coats and wearing a red shirt. I thought he was about the coolest looking thing I had ever seen just walking.

He came right over to us and shook our hands and said, "Guys, I hope you enjoyed the evening. I sure have."

We chatted just a few seconds, and then his handlers moved him on out. Well, when those people down at the stage door saw Elvis, here came the whole mob running, screaming, and hollering. My baritone singer said, "Look a yonder; look who is running up here right in the middle of all of them."

That's right. It was my wife Joy. I teased her about that for years and years.

In addition to raising our children, Joy owned and managed a daycare business for 20 years. After that she went to work for the city, again doing daycare type work through the city's recreation department. Joy was a fantastic seamstress as well.

Here's a funny story about my wife that relates to Elvis and her gift of sewing. A few years ago, I went to answer the door and there was a handsome dude standing there. He had black hair and a little mullet back there, I mean he was sharp as a tack. I was thinking, "What are you doing here at my house?"

He said, "Is your wife in?"

I said, "Yes sir."

He introduced himself and said he needed to talk to Joy about something he wanted her to do. Joy was in her sewing room, so I took him back there. They met and talked for a few minutes. It turned out he was an Elvis impersonator. He said, "Somebody told me if anybody could do it, you could. I don't have a pattern, but I'd like to have this outfit right here made."

He handed her a picture of one of those fancy Elvis jumpsuits like he used to wear on stage. So, Joy made it, and a couple or three weeks later he came back to get it. He was tickled to death.

Two weeks later he came back. I thought he must have liked it so much he's ready to have her make another outfit, but he said to me, "Boy, I hate to ask her this, but I need Mrs. Joy to do something for me."

He had a package in his hand with that jumpsuit in it. He went back and said, "Mrs. Joy, I hate to ask you this, but is there any way you could tighten this up in the thighs a little more?"

She said, "Oh, yes. You won't even have to come back. I can do it right now while you're here."

Joy was a talented lady when it came to something like that.

My wife loved to travel, and with me always on the road, she was able to go with us from time to time especially after the kids were grown and out of the house. She was my inspiration and the only reason I was ever able to follow this dream of singing for an entire lifetime.

She was very independent about her time and always found some way to occupy herself when I was traveling. She loved to sew costumes for plays.

I'll never forget a few years before she passed away, I'd done my office work and got my deposit ready one day. I said, "Baby, I'm gone to the golf course. I'll see you about four o'clock."

She said, "I need to talk to you."

I knew when she said that, something was coming up, you know! She said, "Ed, you're gone all the time, and then when you're home, you're on the golf course. We need to spend more time together."

I said, "OK."

She said, "We need to set aside one day to spend together every week."

I said, "That's fine, but don't pick Monday."

So, we settled on Tuesday.

In the meantime, they were having a big pageant at the church for Easter, and Joy was making the costumes for a cast that numbered about 200! On those Tuesdays, we ended up going all over North Carolina looking at material.

She researched everything to make sure the costumes looked authentic. She'd check on details like what part of the Holy Land they wore this or that. Every Tuesday, we'd hit the road to go to another series of cloth stores

One day I was sitting in the car in a parking lot in Greensboro, North Carolina, and I was listening to Rush Limbaugh on the radio while Joy was in one of those fabric stores. When she came out, I said, "Honey, I want you to know I'm really enjoying these date days!"

We had a good laugh about that. She sure was something else. She rode the bus with me and the group a good bit after she retired. Those were special times.

Joy's health began to decline a few years ago, and she passed away in 2016 on July 10 which was just six days after our 60th wedding anniversary.

In July of 2014, two years before Joy passed away, Melissa Brady wrote a nice article for *Singing News* magazine featuring Joy called "Married to The Music." Joy's memory wasn't always fresh by that point, so our daughter Dara O'Neal Bass answered the interview questions on her behalf.

I appreciate Melissa sharing Joy's story with the readers. Most all of them had probably seen me on stage and a lot of them had talked to me and felt like they knew me. Before that article was printed, though, I doubt many of them realized or even thought about how important it was to have the loyal support of my family and especially my spouse.

Melissa also made room in her article for a short quote from me about Joy, and this is what I said, "She made it easy for me. I never heard the words 'Don't go.' She's been there for me in everything I do, without complaint, and I could not have been out here this long without her support. She's now retired and has traveled with me for the last three years. We're still in love. What a wonderful way to end a career!"

I really do miss her.

Joy O'Neal

Chapter Eleven: Awards and Testimonials

This chapter is going to mostly feature comments from some of the boys who have been members of the Dixie Melody Boys down through the years. I asked a few of them to just share whatever they would like about our time together, whether it's a funny story or just a few memories.

First, though, I want to just quickly mention some awards I've received. I don't want you to think I'm bragging on myself. I've already said I'm the world's worst self-promoter. I am just bringing them up so I can say how grateful I am for the times in my career when an organization has expressed their appreciation for what I've tried to do.

It has always been a tremendous encouragement, and that's true whether it comes directly from the fans or whether it comes from some of my peers who are out here on the road doing the same thing that I'm doing.

The first notable recognition the Dixie Melody Boys received was the Grammy nomination for our album *Sending Up Some Boards* (1978). That was so special to us at the time. We did not win, but I felt like it was a great honor just for us to have been nominated.

Another award the group received came about a year after I'd put a traditional quartet back on the road after I dissolved the DMB Band. Even though we had been around since the 1960s, we were nominated for the Horizon Group category in the *Singing News* Fan Awards in 1988. Our fans voted for us, and we won it. It really helped to re-establish our identity among the fans as a traditional Southern Gospel quartet.

The next award I want to mention was a complete surprise to me. The year was 2000, and I was sitting with my wife Joy in Freedom Hall in Louisville, Kentucky there near the entry where you go down to the stage. It was the week of the National Quartet Convention, and they were presenting the *Singing News* Fan Awards.

I was relaxed and enjoying the program. I had my coat off and my tie undone. They started talking about some guy who had done this and that, and I looked at Joy and said, "It sounds about like they're talking about me, don't it?"

She said, "Yes, it really does."

They kept on and said, "Our recipient tonight is Ed O'Neal."

I went to putting my tie on and grabbing my coat as quickly as I could. That was a total surprise. They presented me with the Marvin Norcross Award.

Another special honor came when the Southern Gospel Music Association (SGMA) inducted me into their Hall of Fame in 2004. That was the same year they inducted Derrell Stewart, London Parris, Jim Hamill, and several other individuals I consider to be legends in Southern Gospel. It was special to be included as part of the same class as those well-known inductees.

Something I said a few weeks before when I found out I was going to be inducted into the SGMA Hall of Fame is kind of funny. I had come in from the golf course one day and was sitting there having a Coca-Cola and watching the news when the phone rang. I picked it up and it was Charlie Waller who headed up the SGMA at that time.

We chatted for a while. Then Charlie said, "Ed, I'm calling to tell you that you're going to be inducted into the SGMA Hall of Fame."

Well, I thought it was a joke, knowing how much Charlie liked to play pranks. He kept on, and I said, "Charlie, you're not serious, are you?"

He said, "I'm very serious. That's the reason I called you."

Now when something like that happens, my mind goes off to some other place. I might say something that makes no sense. I said, "You mean to tell me I'm going to be inducted into the living category?"

Charlie laughed and said, "If you live till October, yes."

We still get a good chuckle out of that memory.

Speaking of the "living category," I've received several awards over the years that had "living legend" in the title. The first was the Naomi Sego Living Legend Award that a magazine presented to me in Pigeon Forge. Another was the SGMA Living Legend Award. I was also given the JD Sumner Living Legend Award.

One other event where I was blessed to be honored was called "Ed O'Neal This Is Your Life." That was held during the Grand Ole Gospel Reunion that Charlie Waller promoted for many years in Greenville, South Carolina as well as a few other locations around the country.

It just makes me feel good when someone notices what I've tried to do with my music career. I want to acknowledge that.

Now I'm done talking about awards. Most of the rest of this chapter will be written by some of the guys who got their start in music singing with the Dixie Melody Boys. Before we get to the guys though, I want to include this nice tribute written by my publicist Deana Surles Warren. Deana is practically my second daughter.

Deana Surles Warren
"My Tribute to Ed O'Neal"
I must have been around 10 years old the first time I ever saw Ed O'Neal and The Dixie Melody Boys. My mom, who has always been a Southern Gospel Music lover, took me to all the local concerts in Eastern North Carolina. Little did I know the impact and lifelong friendship we would develop the first time I ever met him. Over the next six or seven years I would see Mr. Ed and his popular quartet from time to time as we attended concert after concert each time all the popular groups came to our area.

During my senior year of high school, I chose to pursue a degree in Broadcast Journalism from a small two-year college in Kinston, North Carolina, about 75 miles from my home. When my mom and I visited the college, we learned that at the time the school did not offer on-campus housing.

The only people we knew in the town where the college was located were Ed O'Neal and The Dixie Melody Boys. After our visit to the campus and upon learning of the housing situation, we drove across town to where The Dixie Melody Boys' office was located. (I am so glad that many groups at the time placed their addresses on the back of their album covers, and I pretty much memorized all the album covers.)

As we arrived, we were greeted by the group's secretary at the time, Teresa, Ed's daughter-in-law. We began to share our situation with Teresa when Mr. Ed walked in the room. While I'm not sure he really knew who we were, nonetheless, he welcomed us and treated us like we were longtime friends.

As we shared our dilemma with him and Teresa, he said, "Give me just a minute."

He walked back into his office, picked up the phone and within less than five minutes, walked back into where we were waiting.

"Go see Mr. Groff at his wallpaper place. He has a lot of rental places. Even some of my boys (members of The Dixie Melody Boys) rent from him. He typically doesn't rent to college students, but I told him you were a good one," he said with a wink and a big grin.

Later that fall when I started college, I often stopped by The Dixie Melody Boys' office. Ed and his sweet wife, Joy, became like a second mom and dad to me. Their daughter, Dara, and I became good friends. At least one night a week, sometimes more, I could be found on Harding Avenue at the O'Neal home.

A few years after graduating from college, I moved to Boone, NC where another great man, Maurice Templeton, took a chance on me when he offered me a position with his travel agency, Templeton Tours and the Southern Gospel Music publication he had recently purchased, *The Singing News Magazine*.

Over the next seven years I had the privilege of serving on the Magazine's staff, eventually becoming Managing Editor for the publication. In the fall of 1995, I decided to leave *The Singing News* in order to move back to my hometown, where my parents live. My dad had been diagnosed with colon cancer and at the time, the prognosis was not good. With the blessing of Maurice and Jerry Kirksey, the publication's Editor-In-Chief, I moved back home. At the time, I had no idea the career direction my life would take, but I knew the Lord was leading me to make the move.

A few weeks after moving home, I went to a concert where The Dixie Melody Boys were singing. After the service I waited around to visit with Mr. Ed and the guys. After the majority of the people had left, Mr. Ed came over and sat down on the pew where I was sitting.

"What's this I hear about you leaving *The Singing News*," Ed asked in his deep voice with a tone that only a caring dad can have.

"It's true," I replied.

"Well, what are you gonna do," he inquired.

"I have absolutely no idea," I said.

"Honestly, I'm thinking about starting my own publicity company," I continued.

As I shared my ideas and the plans I had that, quite honestly, I had only shared with a few people, I noticed a big grin come upon his face. When I finished, he waited a moment.

"Well when you get it all figured out, give me a call. Whatever you're gonna do, I want to be in on it," he said with a wink and a big grin - the same wink and grin that I had seen more than a decade earlier.

Ed O'Neal will never know how encouraging those words were to me - to think that a true Southern Gospel Music legend believed that much in me and my abilities. Words can't express how much that meant.

In January of 1996, Writer's Ink Publishing opened for business. Ed O'Neal was my very first client. It's 24 years later and Writer's Ink Publishing still represents Ed O'Neal and The Dixie Melody Boys. Over the years I have had the privilege of serving and representing many of Christian's finest recording artists, companies and organizations.

Many individuals have played a major role in the success of Writer's Ink Publishing and Deana Surles Warren. I am forever grateful for the relationships I have enjoyed and for the blessings God has provided. God has used many individuals to afford me with great opportunities; however, I must admit, I will never forget the first man who said "Whatever you're gonna do, I want to be in on it."

Thank you, Ed O'Neal!
I love you!
Deana Surles Warren

Jamey Ragle
I joined the Dixie Melody Boys in 1976 and stayed for almost three years. It was the realization of a dream come true for me. I left my home in Cincinnati, moved to Kinston, North Carolina, and spent three of the happiest years of my life there.

When I was a kid, I used to watch the *Gospel Singing Jubilee*. I would take an empty toilet paper roll and pretend that it was a microphone. I loved to sing along with all the people on the show, so that is why I say my time with the Dixie Melody Boys was the realization of a dream. To be able to sing at the National Quartet Convention, the Wheeling Jamboree, state fairs, many churches, and all those wonderful events was absolutely the pinnacle of excitement for me.

I remember being so nervous when I went to audition. I had this little squeaky tic in my voice. In between songs, I sounded like a mouse squeaking. I never seemed to outlive that. The guys ribbed me about it for many, many years.

I was the clown of the outfit. I enjoyed making people laugh. I was certainly not the best tenor singer, but I did give it my all. I really enjoyed those few years and met some folks who are still my friends even to this day.

Ed is a true legend. He was like a second father to me. All of us who had the privilege to sing with Ed were blessed beyond measure. The investment he made in my life was eternal, and I will be forever grateful.

Jamey Ragle

Frank Sutton
I remember it like it was yesterday. Almost a year after graduating from high school, I was playing bass for Gaylon Pope & the Majestics. We were opening on a Thursday night outside of my hometown, Goldsboro, NC, at the Charles B. Aycock High School gym for one of my family's favorite groups, the Dixie Melody Boys.

After the concert, I was approached by Allen O'Neal and asked if I'd like to try out with the band. We finished and he went to talk to his dad, owner and bass singer Ed O'Neal. He offered me the job. I went to talk to my Dad to which he said "Son, it's what you've been wanting to do for a long time, go for it!"

I quit my job the next day and left on my first of many tours the next week. That night changed the trajectory of my life and is something I still get to enjoy the benefits of to this day. We reap the sown seeds from Ed as Jackson Heights today.

There were so many great years from days of music and memories. Playing in a Kansas stadium at an all-night sing, the PTL network, Will Rogers Auditorium with lots of our heroes like the Happy Goodmans, Cathedrals, Hoppers, Hemphills, and Hinsons, and the list goes on and on!

The laughs we had were innumerable: from putting mustard on anyone's tongue that might have dosed off in the front lounge with their mouth gaped open to scaring someone to death if they had fallen asleep while sitting up with whoever was driving the bus by tapping the brakes and yelling, "LOOK OUT!" That was often me having the heart attack!!

Even the state fairs are still great memories, especially the one where I passed out during the show. Ed still gave his 4 for $10 record pitch while I was on the floor next to him! Gotta love it!

Ed was/is like a father to all of us who had the great fortune to be taken into EOU (Ed O'Neal University). Sometimes it was a school of hard knocks, but what a great teacher of life's lessons. His tutelage and protection of us growing as young men was a Godsend. His sacrifice along with Mrs. Joy's was a gift that none of us can ever pay back. But that is so similar to God's gift of Jesus Christ, our Savior that we don't deserve, can't earn, and can never repay.

So, thank you Ed & Mrs. Joy for making a way for us to live our dreams, for the time you shared with us, and the harvest we still get to enjoy today!

Love ya, Ed!
Frank Sutton

Ricky Horrell
I joined Dixie Melody Boys in August of 1983 and played drums with the band until end of December of 1984. I remember many highlights traveling with some of the best musicians in all of Country Gospel Music!! It was a dream come true when I tried out and got hired the first weekend out on the road. Some of the greatest memories of my whole entire life are from traveling with Ed O'Neal and all of the DMB Band.

The first weekend out we played at Kempton, Pennsylvania at an annual outdoor concert where there were over 2000 people there on that Sunday. WOW it was an AWESOME experience for my first weekend out on the road with the boys!!

We were on the bus many days and nights; 10-day trips, 15-day trips, and sometimes 21 days out on the road!! We would leave our concert and travel all night to the next date, and we took 2-hour shifts to stay up with the driver. We would get up and sit in the buddy seat near the driver to help keep them awake. Ed, Allen, and Craig would switch out driving.

One particular time, I remember Allen was to start driving, and it was my turn to stay up with him. We were getting fuel. After that, we would go in a truck stop, and we both would get a big honeybun, and let them put it in a microwave, and then we would put butter on it, and eat it on a plate with a fork. It was some kinda good.

After that, we went back on the bus and rode for around 2 hours later. It was then time to wake up Jerry Kelso. I went to his bunk, but he was not there!

We looked all over the bus and could not find him. As you know there were no cell phones back in those days, so we figured he got off the bus at the truck stop and didn't tell anyone and he got left behind. We had to backtrack 2 hours and pick him up, so then it made us 4 hours behind that night! Ed had a "let's go to meeting" with Jerry, and from that night on, he never got off the bus again without letting someone know first.

We all had to go to the School of Allen O'Neal when it came to cord rolling. There was only one way to roll up cords and pack them up, and that was the way Allen wanted them. We all learned from the BEST!!

One big highlight I remember was when we played on the same concert stage with The Imperials and Mylon LeFevre & Broken Heart. The auditorium was a sold-out crowd, and we started the program off that night with our County Gospel or Middle of the Road blend of music. We won the crowd that night, and it was just AWESOME, and a great feeling to be on same stage with those amazing artists!! We Rocked the house that night with our music!!

Another great thing during that time was our number one song which was "Good Ole Boys." Also, during this time frame, we were voted number one band in Gospel music 2 years in a row. That was an HONOR to play drums with such talent as the DMB BAND had!! They don't get any better. Ed, Allen, Kent, Frank, Craig, and Jerry were the best musicians and singers, and also friends and were like family!! I will always cherish my time spent on the road with THE DMB BAND!!!

Ricky Horrell

Kent Humphrey
How do I start to talk about my time on the road with Ed O'Neal? I was a 17-year-old kid with big dreams of singing Southern Gospel Music as a career. I was singing with my dad's group at the time and we opened a concert for the Dixie Melody Boys at my home church in Greensburg, KY.

That night I got up the nerve to give my name and number to Ron Wells, their steel guitarist and said, "If you guys ever need a lead singer, I would love the opportunity to audition."

The very next week their lead singer resigned, and I got the call to come and audition for the job in Ypsilanti, Michigan. My dad drove me there. We listened to their concert that night and then around midnight, I got the chance to audition.

Ed came to my hotel room that night after the audition and offered me the job with my dad's permission of course! This was on a Thursday night and he said, "Meet us in Louisville,

Kentucky on Sunday night with all your stuff and hop on the bus."

So that's what I did! Ed saw something in a 17-year-old kid and gave him a chance to live out his dream!

Ed was always like a dad to all of us guys on the road. In the music business, people don't always live the lives that you perceive, but Ed O'Neal did, and he made sure that his guys did as well.

I started with the group when the name was the Dixie Melody Boys and was there through the DMB Band era. We saw great times and we walked through seasons that were rough, but we were a family! Ed always made every singer and musician feel that they were part of this special family.

Ed's famous line was "All I ever wanted to do is sing a song". That sounds simple but in the music business it takes commitment, tenacity, perseverance and integrity just to be able to make that happen! My 7 years on the road with Ed were something that I wouldn't trade, and it prepared me for a life in the world of music.

Thank You Ed for believing in me as a young man! I have had a lot of heroes in my life, but you, my friend, are a legend in my book!

Kent Humphrey

Larry DeLawder

Ed was like a dad to me. I learned a lot from him, and I'm so thankful for the opportunity he gave to an 18-year-old boy! We had a lot of fun on the bus and in concerts. His stories were legendary! Ed is a big part of who I am today. His investment in my life is something I'm so grateful for.

Even at that, if it wasn't for "Mama Joy," I wouldn't have had those 8½ years with the Dixie Melody Boys.

In 1987, my family was in Gettysburg, Pennsylvania hosting concerts at a campground after many years traveling on the road. We had been in concert with Ed in the DMB Band days, and then had them in to the campground for a concert. Somehow Ed had gotten the number for the campground and called me about my brother and me being a part of the group. I remember the day Ed & Rayburn Lane picked us up in that old yellow Lincoln!

After we got back to North Carolina, Ed realized I couldn't play quartet style piano, so he was going to send me home & keep my brother. Mama Joy stepped in and said, "Edward, that boy needs you!"

I am so very grateful. Whether she knew it or not, the Lord used her to help shape my future because of my time with Ed and the boys. Ed decided to keep me on while featuring me on harmonica and percussion.

There are many things he taught me (and everyone else who has gone through "Ed O'Neal University")! One of the most impactful bits of wisdom he shared was the day he said, "Larry, if you'd cut out about half of what you're playing, you'd be a great harmonica player."

This simple truth along with him featuring me in every concert and service allowed me to be nominated several times for instrumentalist of the year in a category only previously known for piano players, and then go on to win the Hearts Aflame award. I owe that all to Ed, because he believed in me and pushed me to be my best!

Larry DeLawder

McCray Dove

In 1987, I auditioned for the Dixie Melody Boys. I can still remember it scene by scene in my mind and still feel the excitement as I recall that day that changed my life. I remember hearing Ed tell my mother, "Miss Dove don't you worry. I'll treat him just like he was my son."

That's exactly what Ed did. I learned so much about singing and managing a quartet from Ed, but more importantly, Ed taught me about life. Integrity was very important to Ed. He believed in walking the walk and talking the talk. He'd say, "Show more with your actions than your words."

There was a song Ed wrote that he would recite to us when he was wanting to get his point across. I have made it part of my walk in life. From time to time, I recite it to myself to remind me what I need to do.

There are those who will say with their lips, "I love Jesus."
Those who will say, "He is mine."
Others will shout and sing of His praise,
But for souls, they never have time.

If you have the love of Christ in your heart.
You will show it, you see.
Tell me one time you love Jesus.
Tell me one time, then show me.

McCray Dove

Rodney Griffin
I sang with Ed and The Dixie Melody Boys for two years…1992 and 1993. I had come from singing with the Brashears in Russellville, Arkansas. When I moved to Kinston, I suddenly found myself singing on the largest stages in Gospel Music…and Ed was the reason.

My heroes were Glen Payne and George Younce and now I found myself visiting with them at sound check and sitting on the bus hearing their stories…all because of Ed. I noticed how much they respected Ed and looked at him as a steady contributor to Gospel Music. I remember Glen Payne coming up on our bus when the Cathedrals' *High and Lifted Up* CD, produced by Lari Goss was "in the can." Glen was so very proud of this recording and wanted Ed to hear it. He respected Ed's opinion. He also took time to brag on "Ed's boys." Glen enjoyed Ed's fervor for this music and was happy to have him as a friend.

Everywhere we sang, what I saw was a deep respect for Ed by all the other artists we worked with. All the while, I saw Dixie Melody Boys' fans waiting to talk to Ed every night…and he would patiently give them each time to visit. He is loved and admired by all who ever sang in his group, by all the other artists who ever shared the stage with him, and by every fan who has ever sat out there and enjoyed his smooth bass voice.

What I most admire about Ed is his continued friendship after all these years. You know you are friends when it's not unusual to see his name come up on your caller ID. I am so very honored to have shared the stage with him at the start of my career.

He believed in me back then even as an unproven young singer. He was a part of my first song ever recorded, "I Have A New Song to Sing," written for our live album that we recorded in Marion, Illinois. He then included two of my songs, "I Won't Compromise" and "When My Knees Touch Gold," on our next project. He encouraged me as a young writer.

I'll never forget the opportunity he gave me and the memories we made on the bus together. He's exactly what you see. A gentleman…and to me…a true hero.

Thanks Ed!
Rodney Griffin

Matt Felts

I had been singing for a few years when Ed O'Neal called me and asked me to join the Dixie Melody Boys. I was walking through a store when he called, but when his name popped up on my phone, I stopped in my tracks. I asked him when he wanted me to come audition. He replied, "McCray Dove gave me your name and said you could do the job. That's all I need to know. When can you start?"

I was on a plane three days later to meet the bus. When I walked onto that bus, I had no idea how much my time with Ed would shape the rest of my life.

I quickly learned why Ed O'Neal has given the Gospel world so many great artists. He has a gift for sensing someone's talent, and then giving them an opportunity to showcase that talent.

Ed saw in me a desire to get behind the scenes of the Southern Gospel world and help with the business side of the group. He allowed me to take the reins of our promotion, marketing, and much of the day to day business. He allowed me to be the face of our group in meetings, a role that most group owners would never relinquish.

Ed spent hours on the bus, on a golf course, or at his table over dinner mentoring me and sharing the wisdom that helped him stay on the road for many years. He told me about how important relationships were and to always appreciate the fans and pastors that support us. While many of his lessons came in conversation, most came just from watching how he conducted his business and his life.

I had been with the DMBs about a year when *The Singing News* decided to honor the group's 50th anniversary at the National Quartet Convention. Ed and I talked about the best way to celebrate that milestone. After deciding to do a reunion with as many of the former members as we could gather, Ed turned it over to me to organize. One by one, I called each former member to invite them to Louisville.

By the time we arrived at the Convention, over 30 former members were in attendance. We met the night before the Reunion to rehearse. As we waited on everyone to arrive, guys started swapping stories about their time with the Dixie Melody Boys. Each story revolved around Ed O'Neal. I also heard thirty different impersonations of Ed's Carolina accent as they told story after story and quoted the boss.

When Ed walked into the room, the guys all clapped and rushed to greet him with a hug. Seeing the love each of the alumni had for him was a testimony to his career. It's one thing for fans to love you, but it means more when the men who watched your testimony everyday love you also.

The next day, Ed spoke to the crowd and took the time to acknowledge my work putting the event together. Many people would just take the credit for themselves, but once again, Ed O'Neal wanted the attention to go to his boys.

Since leaving the Dixie Melody Boys, I've had the honor to sing with other groups such as the Lesters and transition deeper into the business side of music, owning my own company, Gateway Management. I've been blessed to work with artists such as Larry Gatlin, the Oak Ridge Boys, Darryl Worley, baseball legend Don Mattingly, and tour with Christian Music icon Carman, serving as his manager.

How did all of this happen? This journey all started with a phone call from Ed O'Neal. My life would never be the same.

I'll close with a special story about Ed.

In the fall of 2011, we were scheduled to sing on a Sunday in Mississippi for a church homecoming. We arrived at the church early so we could set up our sound for the morning service. It was a crisp fall day and there was fog rolling across the parking lot.

The church set on top of a hill with the church fellowship building down the hill across the parking lot. As we went into the sanctuary, Ed walked down the hill to the fellowship hall hoping to find some coffee. A few minutes had passed when Steven Cooper came rushing into the back of the church and yelled to me, "Ed has fallen, and it's bad."

I ran out of the church and saw Ed lying on the pavement in between the church and our bus. As I got closer, I could see blood and knew he was in bad shape. Ed had looked for coffee, didn't find any and was on his way back to the bus. He exited a side door and began to walk out.

What he didn't know was the church had removed the steps and were planning on replacing them later that week. Ed stepped out and before he could realize what was happening, he fell six feet down to the pavement below!

The church offered to take him to the hospital. I wanted to go with him, but he insisted we stay and sing in the first service. We also had an afternoon concert scheduled. Without Ed, we did our best to make it through the first service. In the break between services, Ed arrived with a leg brace on and bandages on his head and hand. As I got him on the bus, I tried to get him to lay down in his bunk. He said, "I'm singing. Help me get dressed."

Wow! He had every reason to skip the singing. Everyone would have understood. Ed wouldn't have it.

With the use of a cane and sitting on a stool, Ed O'Neal gave one of the most powerful concerts I've ever been a part of. Knowing that Ed was in incredible pain, the audience saw just how deep his desire to sing for Jesus was. That experience was such a perfect example of his whole career. It was oftentimes difficult to keep a group on the road, but Ed never gave up. He gave everything he had.

Matt Felts

Josh Garner
I love Ed O' Neal. From the first time I met him as a 15-year-old boy, I loved him. Outside of my family, it is arguable that Ed has been my biggest cheerleader in Gospel music. He

believed in me from the very beginning and hasn't stopped encouraging me to this day.

Like a lot of DMB alumni, I feel like I could write an entire book on our adventures together. I would love to tell of the countless hours we have laughed and cried together or the many times we have seen the Lord work in each of our lives. However, I want to share a side of Ed that a lot of people may not know about and the love of his life for over 60 years.

The very first time I saw Ed O' Neal in person, I was terrified of him. I was a big, strapping 15-year-old, but Ed was larger than life. When he sauntered, and I do mean sauntered, into the Wayne City High School auditorium in Wayne City, Illinois where I and my family group would open a concert for the legendary Dixie Melody Boys, I was star struck.

I didn't know the history of the DMB too well and had never seen them in concert, but I knew Ed's reputation as a great quartet man and a tremendous singer, and I was extremely nervous to meet him. Just the way he dressed and carried himself, he looked like a star.

I know it's hard to believe, but by nature, I am a shy person. I honestly don't even know if I talked to him before the concert, because he just made me nervous. However, after the program was over, like many singers before me and many after, I became one of Ed's "buddies." He offered me a job that night, not knowing my age, and assured me that one day I would be a Dixie Melody Boy. It took 20 years for that to happen, but I'm so glad it did.

It was early summer of 2013, and I had been doing pretty well with a group John Rulapaugh and I started called Freedom.

John was very involved in some other business ventures and wanted to scale back from singing, but I still wanted to make Gospel music my career. The Lord never ceases to amaze me with His timing, because it was around this time that I got the call from DMB. Mind you, it was the eighth call in 20 years, but this time it was just right. Ed was in a bind and needed a lead singer right away. I told him I could fill in when Freedom wasn't working, but I couldn't stay.

I knew that Mama Joy was now traveling with Ed because of her Alzheimer's diagnosis, so I could only imagine the added stress Ed was under, and I wanted to help him out since he'd always been so good to me.

It only took a few weeks for Ed and me both to realize that I needed to join the group full-time. Over the next six years, the initial image I had of Ed O' Neal as a gruff, intimidating task master of sorts transformed into one of a man who was the most tender hearted, compassionate, loving caregivers I've ever known.

If a man ever loved his wife, Ed O' Neal loved and adored his high school sweetheart, Joy Marie. I had heard many stories through the years of how Mama Joy was the ultimate quartet wife and how she took care of Ed's boys, but I never got to meet that woman. By the time I joined the group, Joy was firmly in the grip of Alzheimer's.

I'm certain she never knew who I or any of the other boys were, but she understood that we were supposed to be there. In my first year with the group, I studied Ed as he tried to figure out how to handle the little episodes Joy would have, and my heart ached as he would exhaust himself trying to meet her needs.

He eventually got the hang of it, but it was definitely a team effort. We all pitched in to give Ed some much needed rest. There were several lighter moments, though. I'll never forget the advice Jeff Easter gave to all of us. Jeff lost his mother to Alzheimer's and he said, "Boys, if you don't laugh at the silly stuff, you'll just cry all the time."

Every time we worked with the Easters, Jeff would sneak up behind Joy and say, "Mama Joy, you want to go smoke?"

With a disgusted look, Joy would reply, "I don't smoke!"

Then Jeff would say, "We just did five minutes ago!"

Joy would put her hand up in his face and wave him off. For the record, Jeff Easter doesn't smoke, but it was little things like this that gave Ed a chance to enjoy the situation and see a glimpse of the witty woman he married. In addition to the comic relief, Jeff told us that anything we could do to occupy her mind was good for her. We found this to be true. Joy would often wander off and one of us would have to chase her down. She was always looking for something or someone. If she asked once, she would ask 1,000 times a day, "Where's Edward?"

One day as she was roaming the bus asking for Edward, I remembered what Jeff had said. I got Joy's attention and she asked again, "Where's Edward?"

I simply looked at her and said, "He's upstairs."

Bless her heart, she looked for those stairs for nearly an hour, but it kept her occupied and focused on something.

My first trip to Salisbury, Maryland was a memorable one. This was an annual date for the DMB that was normally held outside, but due to rain was moved indoors. Everyone was seated at long rows of tables and it was unusual, but we made it work. Near the end of the concert, Ed looked over and asked if I knew "Happy Rhythm." I said, "Of course," so he set it up.

As soon as the music hit, Joy, who was seated right in the middle of these rows of tables got up and started dancing up and down the aisles. We couldn't sing for laughing so hard.

Ed's face was bright red and he was doubled over with laughter. As the song ended, Joy made her way up to the makeshift stage so everyone could see her. She got a standing ovation and then she took a bow. I have never seen an audience so overcome with sheer and literal Joy!

That was the most memorable onstage escapade, but to me the funniest Ed and Joy moment happened on the bus one afternoon. As we often would, all the boys and Joy had gathered in the front lounge of the bus just talking. It was about an hour before show time, so that meant it was time for Ed to get ready. He patted Mama Joy on the knee and said, "Come on, Mama, I'm going to get dressed."

Joy replied with a shocked look, "You're going to do what?"

Ed said, "I'm going to get dressed."

Now with a look of disgust, Joy responded, "You're going to put on a dress?"

We all chuckled, and Ed said with a louder, exasperated tone, "No, Mama, I'm going to get dressed!"

Joy just shook her head as Ed made his way to the back of the bus. Then she looked at the rest of us and said disdainfully, "He's a sissy!"

We were rolling in the floor.

As the Alzheimer's got worse, the laughter ceased, and it became almost too much for Ed to bear. He barely ate, he never slept, but he was by her side each and every second of every day. I can't express enough how difficult it is caring for someone with Alzheimer's and only those who have experienced it can relate.

Add to that fact that every night Ed would put on that suit and that smile to encourage and entertain all the folks that would come out to see him, when in reality, he was the one in need of uplifting. But somehow, with the Lord's help, he did it.

The stress and fatigue finally took its toll when we were in Nashville for a photo shoot. It was a long shoot and when we finally wrapped, I went to the bus to change clothes and I saw Ed in his room shivering like he was freezing. I hollered, "Are you cold, buddy?"

His color had turned gray and he replied that he wasn't cold. but he couldn't stop shaking. We immediately took him to a nearby emergency room, but he fought us the whole way because he didn't want to leave Joy. Here was a man who was completely exhausted, dehydrated and malnourished in need of medical care, but his only concern was his wife. We assured him that we would take care of Joy until their kids could make it to Nashville, but he worried about her all night.

I really must take this time to mention Rayburn Lane, Aaron Dishman, Doug Pittman, Steven Cooper, Danny Jones, and Rick Francis, not just for this episode but for all the many things they did for Ed and Joy. People will never know the lengths these men went to, but I know, and God knows. I'm certain they will have a few extra stars in their heavenly crowns.

Yes, my time with the Dixie Melody Boys was unorthodox to say the least, but I know that God placed me there at that time for a very specific reason and for that, I am honored. Not only did I finally get to sing with my "buddy," but I got to witness firsthand a biblical marriage lived out before my very eyes.

There aren't enough words to express my admiration and respect for Ed O'Neal, not simply because of his contributions to the Kingdom of God through Gospel music, but mostly for the way he loved his wife and the example he set for all of us.

He is a living legend, a Hall of Famer, and one of the greatest singers Gospel music has ever known. Better than all that, though, Ed O' Neal loves his Lord, he loves his wife to this day, and he is loved by all those who know him. All he ever wanted to do is sing a song, and I'm so thankful I got to sing a few with him.

I love you, Boss Man!
Josh Garner

Jerry Skaggs

I sang tenor for the Dixie Melody Boys from May 2017 through June 2019. The DMB were always a favorite of mine. Actually, getting to sing with them and one of the smoothest and most talented basses in the industry was certainly a blessing!

Being the new guy, I often got the opportunity to share hotel rooms with Ed, and I got to know him on a more personal level. I know he truly is an honorable and humble man.

I am thankful for the opportunity I had to sing with him. It was a true blessing to be able to call him boss, and also to be able to still call him friend!

Jerry Skaggs

Willie Sawrey

"The reason I am late, is I did not leave on time!"

That is one of the many "Ed-isms" I learned after joining the Dixie Melody Boys in September of 2016. I was very familiar with the Dixie Melody Boys, having been involved in part-time gospel music for over 25 years.

The call came to me from Ed O'Neal looking for someone to help him fill some dates while he searched for a suitable replacement of a recently departed member. I was extremely honored to be considered as a "fill-in" knowing the high standard of excellence that Ed had always set. Nevertheless, it was a dream come true.

I became a Christian in 1985. My high interest in quartet music was due to seeing the Dixie Melody Boys perform live at my home church in 1988. I felt that the music ministry was something I really wanted to do. I had no idea that one day the opportunity to be a part of the very first full-time quartet I ever saw in person would come my way.

I remember my very first date with Ed O'Neal's Dixie Melody Boys was at the Golden Isles Christian Church in Brunswick, Georgia. I was a bit nervous, especially having to stand right beside Ed who was an award-winning, Southern Gospel Hall of Famer!!! I remember after that first night Ed let me know I did fine and each time would get easier.

The next few weeks did get easier and a mutual respect began to grow. A few weeks passed and the Dixie Melody Boys were at the 2016 National Quartet Convention in Pigeon Forge, Tennessee performing Tuesday and then again on Saturday. Ed was able to get McCray Dove for Tuesday night.

I decided to call on Wednesday and let him know that I was available for the next couple of weeks if he needed someone. He let me know that he didn't have anyone for Saturday, and he had been very concerned not knowing how he was going to perform without a baritone. Without any hesitation, I let him know if he needed me, I would be there. He asked, "How can I get you here?"

I told him I would drive up Friday, get a room and be ready to help on Saturday night. He later let me know he rested well the rest of the week knowing all positions were filled!! The

Dixie Melody Boys had a great set on Saturday night, and I finished the week with them on a Sunday morning in Macon, Georgia.

As we traveled back home to North Carolina, I again let Ed know if he needed me anymore, I was available. He said he would like me to fill in more on a permanent basis. He had offered me the job!! I remember thinking, "I hope he doesn't see my overwhelming excitement on my face," but inside I could barely contain my emotions.

I told him I needed to talk it over with my wife, Dana, and I would let him know. Ed told me right then how important it was to have a wife that understood and supported a gospel singer. After four years singing with the Dixie Melody Boys, the learning has continued. Ed O'Neal is a great encourager, mentor, and supporter of all Southern Gospel music, especially his Dixie Melody Boys. It has been and will always be an honor to be associated with the list of men who have entered the ranks of Ed O'Neal University (EOU)!!!

Willie Sawrey

Chapter Twelve: Road Stories

Road stories are what you're going to hear in a Waffle House after a concert, in a dressing room backstage, on the bus sitting in the lounge area, or just about anywhere else where you might find two or three old quartet guys sitting around and talking.

In this final chapter, I'm going to tell you some of my favorite stories from traveling on the road for the past 60 years or so. A few of these stories are just curious things I've observed, but most are things I've either done or seen that were so funny to me. I hope you enjoy reading them at least as much as I've enjoyed telling them!

She Didn't Like the Kingsmen
Back in the early days, I had a band member whose wife thought she was just too spiritual to enjoy certain groups. She thought a concert should be formal and reverent and she let

it be known to me on more than one occasion that she didn't care for much of nothing else.

I scheduled the Kingsmen Quartet to come sing on my annual homecoming one year, and let me tell you, they were hot as a firecracker in those days. Before the day arrived, my band member's wife, this spiritual-minded girl, told me in no uncertain terms that she thought the Kingsmen were just show business and entertainment. She especially didn't like Jim Hamill. She said he was too boisterous when he sang.

She disliked the Kingsmen so much that when we brought them on stage at my homecoming, she got up and went out to sit in her car so she wouldn't have to watch them. It just so happened she had parked right in front of the Kingsmen's bus, and where she was sitting, she could see inside the bus through the windshield. I don't think she parked there on purpose to look in or anything, but that's just where she happened to be. At any rate, she was still sitting in her car when the Kingsmen wrapped up their part of the program.

Jim Hamill always worked up a sweat on stage and he'd be tired after it was over. He'd often wind down by going out to their bus and putting in a chew of Red Man. He'd sit on the couch leaning forward with his head in his hands spitting tobacco juice into a gallon can on the floor.

That's what he did that day.

Well, this girl saw him. She didn't realize he was spitting Red Man, but she observed him there on the couch with his head in his hands. In a few minutes she came inside with big tears in her eyes and said she wanted to see me. I said, "What's the problem?"

I really thought she was going to lay into me again about bringing in the Kingsmen. She was crying and said, "I just want to apologize to you. I'm so sorry I felt that way about the Kingsmen. When that big guy came off the stage, I saw him get on their bus. He sat down on the couch, and he bowed his head. I bet he prayed for fifteen minutes!"

It had upset her so much, but from then on, the Kingsmen were her number one group!

You Just Got Lucky

One thing I loved about Jim Hamill was his competitive streak. We always tried to top the Kingsmen, and they always tried to top us. The fans always knew they were going to get the best from both groups any time we were scheduled on the same program.

One year when both groups were scheduled to appear on the same night at the National Quartet Convention in Nashville, Hamill and I got together earlier in that day to play golf. All day on the golf course, he said things to me like, "You'd better bring your best singing shoes, O'Neal. You're singing after the Kingsmen, and we're going to mow you down!"

That night, Hamill played that crowd like a violin. They did every Kingsmen hit they could squeeze in the amount of time they had to sing. It took several minutes for the emcee to get the crowd settled down enough to bring us on. As he came off the stage, Hamill gave me a big grin and said, "Your turn, O'Neal! Top that!"

Suddenly, I had an idea. Sometimes in our regular programs, we would imitate groups like the Goffs, the Inspirations, and the Kingsmen. We had never done it at NQC mainly due to the time limit. Given how much Hamill had been getting in my ear all day long, though, I thought it was worth a shot.

We began with our imitations of the Goffs and the Inspirations, and then we took off on "Shake Hands with A Poor Boy." Of course, I played Ray Dean Reese and tried my best to mimic his mannerisms and tone. The audience began cheering, but that was just the beginning.

That's when Frank Sutton was singing with us. Frank was a relatively short guy, but he had developed a great imitation of Hamill. Frank threw his tie in the audience, and his coat went right behind it. Then in the heat of the moment before I realized what he was doing, Frank threw ME into the crowd.

The crowd loved it. I wasn't too crazy about it, though, from the spot where I had landed on the floor in pain. I was able to get up on my knees by the end of the song just as Frank yelled Hamill's famous line to the audience, "You like that kind of singing?"

I didn't try to get back on the stage. I just walked around it, and there stood Jim Hamill waiting for me by the steps. He said if it had been him, he would have landed on his feet. He said Ray could out sing me any day of the week even if he was sick, and that the Kingsmen sounded better than us when they weren't even trying. Then Hamill told me it was the best thing he'd ever seen in all his years coming to the NQC. The last thing he said was, "O'Neal, don't let this go to your head. You just got lucky. I'll get you next time."

I remember another time when we were on the same program as the Kingsmen in Springdale, Arkansas at the rodeo arena for the Brumley Gospel Sing. It was a multi-night event, and Bob Brumley usually booked the same groups on the same nights every year. Friday night was our night, and Friday night was also the Kingsmen's night. They always went on last to close out the show.

Bob had a meeting with us before the show started to tell us how he wanted it to go. Now again, keep in mind that it was a tradition that the Kingsmen always closed the program on Friday night…except that year. I looked at the list and the last two groups were the Kingsmen and the Dixie Melody Boys in that order.

I went and told McCray Dove, "We've got a problem."

He said, "What's that."

I said, "They're singing right before us this year. They're going to try to bury us."

McCray said, "I don't see no problem."

McCray was just as cocky as Jim Hamill was in those days, you know. He went out to the sound guy and ask him to put two wireless microphones on stands on the stage, one for him and one for Larry DeLawder. He told him to be ready on the last song. We had known the sound guy for years, and he was more than happy to help. In addition to running sound, he was also a drummer. In the past, we had brought him up to join us on stage.

Well, the Kingsmen had a great program that night. They encored "Stand Up" a couple of times and the crowd was into it. The place was rocking as they finished.

We went on next and did our stand. We got to the end and went into our closer, which was "Glory Cloud." After we did it one time, the crowd was excited, so we turned it around for a second time. About halfway through that time, McCray and Larry DeLawder grabbed those two wireless microphones and jumped off the stage. The stage wasn't a low-boy, it was a high-boy.

McCray went so far back in the crowd that he had to quit singing because of the delay. He couldn't hear the beat, but he was still waving that handkerchief. The crowd just ate it up.

Jim Hamill didn't like it when we went to great lengths to upstage them like that. After it was all over, I told McCray to go over and talk to Hamill. I didn't want him to be too mad at us!

Here Comes the Mud

That rodeo arena where the Brumley concerts were held in Springdale, Arkansas that I just mentioned in the previous story could pack in about 10,000 people. It was so dusty that when it rained, the whole place was like one big mud pie. One year, there was probably five inches of mud in the center of the arena. The stage and people with lawn chairs were sinking into the ground. Mud was everywhere!

The fans loved the music so much, though, they got trash bags or any kind of plastic bag they could find to cover their shoes and came on in that muddy place. I never saw an empty seat no matter how much it rained.

When we did the "Glory Cloud" song that was usually our closing number in those days, Larry DeLawder and McCray Dove would do all sorts of crazy stunts like climbing on speakers or jumping off the stage to get closer to the people like I mentioned before. That year it was so muddy, they both forgot about the mud and jumped off the stage like they would anywhere else during "Glory Cloud." Larry had on a pair of loafers, and when they sunk into the mud, that's where they stayed!

In fact, Larry's shoes are probably still there. He ended up in his stocking feet shaking the tambourine and playing that harmonica to finish out the song!

McCray fared a little better. He was wearing cowboy boots, and the boots stayed on when he jumped into the mud. He got excited, though, and kicked his foot in the air. When he did, his boot slung a chunk of mud right into the face of a man who was sitting on the front row. This guy had been sitting there stone-faced the entire time we were singing. He hadn't smiled or laughed or reacted at all to anything we'd done the entire concert.

I didn't know how that man was going to react, but I knew I sure wouldn't be too happy if it had been me who had just been smacked in the head with a big clump of mud. I thought he'd be mad.

This man didn't get upset at all, though. He just took his index finger and wiped all that mud away in one motion, and then he jumped up with both hands in the air shouting, "Woo, Hallelujah!"

Now, here is another mud story for you. We were in Taylor, Florida at an outdoor event with the Lewis Family on a ball field. Each group had already sung on the first half, and it was time to go out and start the second half after intermission.

We heard some thunder off in the distance, and that worried Little Roy Lewis. He said he was nervous about going out there on stage with a bunch of stringed instruments. I said we could go ahead and just leave the mics on the stands.

It had already rained there the day before, and while we were singing, it started raining again. We got to the end and we were closing out with "When I Cross to The Other Side of Jordan," just giving it all we had.

Some of the youth in the crowd were enjoying it so much they started running and sliding in the mud! Some of them were falling down face first sliding into home plate on the ball field. I looked around and the next thing you know, here came the pastor sliding in the mud too!

I'd never seen anything like it. When it was all over, Little Roy Lewis came by laughing and said to me, "Ed, y'all are just as crazy as them people sliding in the mud like a bunch of pigs!"

Jump on Him, Jesus!
Larry DeLawder really was something else, especially when he played the harmonica. When he first joined the group, he liked to play everything fast. Sometimes it was so fast, nobody knew what he was playing, so I started featuring him and had him slow way down.

Larry hadn't been with us that long when we were in Savannah, Georgia at a big, big church that seated about 800 people. It had a high ceiling and some amazing acoustics. I can't remember if it was Baptist or Pentecostal, but both the lower level and the balconies were full.

Now, everyone I saw in the church that day was white people, except down near the front about three or four rows back was a family of four black people. One was an older man, a small guy about the size of McCray Dove, and he had hair that was just as white as cotton. Now, I didn't do this because I saw them sitting there, but it was time in the program where I usually featured Larry. I said, "Larry, come on up here. I want you to play 'Amazing Grace' on that harmonica."

Now back when Larry joined the group and we started to feature him playing "Amazing Grace," I noticed how people reacted when he'd bend those notes. I had told him, "Give it a little more of that."

By the time we got to this church in Georgia, he had it down pat. Larry had that harmonica crying. As he started, the natural reverb just rolled through that big church. After a few seconds, I heard a soft "umm hmm," and I realized it was coming from the man I mentioned with the white hair. As Larry got into it, that little guy started rocking back and forth. He was loving it.

About this point, Larry realized he was getting a reaction and so he just made it sound just as bluesy as he could. Finally, he got it sounding so soulful, that little black man slid completely out of his seat and into the aisle. He just couldn't stay still no longer. He yelled, "Jump on him, Jesus, jump on him!"

The whole place came apart. That's another time I got to laughing so hard on stage that I almost cried.

Is There Time for A Potty Break Before We Sing?
The most embarrassed I ever saw Larry DeLawder happened when we were doing a concert at a ranch. The stage was set up with bleachers out behind where people could sit in lawn chairs.

Porta potties are a necessity at an event like this, but I don't know why the promoter decided to set up a whole row of them right beside the seats. They were in complete view of the singers on the stage as well as the entire audience. Then again, we were at a ranch where a certain aroma was already in the air.

We were waiting for another group to finish so we could go on stage. Larry DeLawder looked at me and said, "Ed, I have to go to the bathroom really bad. Do you think I'll have time to go before we sing?"

I told him to go ahead, because I honestly thought there was enough time. Of course, I also knew if it worked out that there wasn't enough time, it would be something we could laugh about. Sure enough, about two minutes later, just as Larry had about enough time to settle in real good, I heard the emcee say to the crowd there, "Ladies and gentlemen, from Kinston, North Carolina, please make welcome the Dixie Melody Boys!"

We went on stage and started the first song without Larry. I knew the second he opened the door on that potty, everyone in the crowd would see him and know exactly why he was late getting on the stage. From where we were singing, we could see him peek out a couple of times. He was hoping for an opportunity to sneak out when he wouldn't be noticed. We were all trying not to laugh as we were singing.

Larry finally gave up and just walked out. Of course, every head in the crowd immediately turned to stare at him. Now, he could have just walked straight on to the stage, but instead, he went all the way around behind the people and came in the other side, making it that much worse.

That was bad enough, but later that night after the concert the man who had the ranch wanted us all to ride his horses. It was dark by this point and the horse Larry got on immediately took off. Larry kept yelling, "WHOA!" and pulling back on the reins, but he wouldn't stop!

After a while, the horse finally did stop, and Larry was able to get off with nothing hurt but his pride.

You Better Get Some Insurance
Larry DeLawder was known best for playing harmonica, but he could and did play other instruments. One instrument he used on stage for a great effect was the tambourine. When we'd sing "Gonna Ride That Glory Cloud," he had got the timing just right to throw his tambourine way up in the air and catch it when it came down right on the beat. The crowds always loved it.

One night when we were at the National Quartet Convention, we were closing out our set with that song. We had done a couple of encores and we got to that moment where Larry always threw his tambourine, but he wasn't used to all those lights.

When he made his throw way up in the air, he completely lost sight of his tambourine. He had no idea where it was going to land!

Well, when it came down, it hit our tenor singer Derrick Boyd right on the nose and cut him. Derrick walked off the stage bleeding like he had been in a boxing match.

The Bishops were coming up on stage next. Kenny Bishop told the crowd as we were coming down, "Y'all be sure to come see those guys again, but you better get you some insurance first!"

Mr. Taylor Didn't Like Gospel Music

Back in the early days, I partnered with a company called Wheeling Talent Agency. They scheduled us to perform on a lot of fairs around the country during the summer months. At one fair in West Virginia, there was a Mr. Taylor that I reported to and he did not like Gospel music. Period.

Therefore, he did not like me, and he did not like the Dixie Melody Boys. I'm not sure what his title was exactly, because he didn't book the groups for this fair. We just had to report to him when we got there like I mentioned.

We got there, and all he had provided for us to stand on was a concrete slab. No stage, just a slab of concrete there on the ground. He said, "That's where you're gonna sing."

We started setting up there and it started raining. The forecast was calling for a lot of rain, so we just took it back down. He said, "Well, I guess you won't be giving us none of that gospel music today."

I said, "Well, I don't know yet."

Mr. Taylor said, "If you don't sing, you don't get paid."

I saw some Amish ladies up the hill at a barn. They had a lean-to on the side of the barn with some quilts hanging up there on display. I went up and said, "Ladies, we're supposed to sing down on that concrete slab, but it's raining so bad. Is there any way we could move your quilts back and sing under this shelter? We'll be finished and out of the way again in about 45 minutes."

They said, "Sure, we'll be glad to help you do it."

So, we did our program there, and it made Mr. Taylor so mad. After we were finished, I said, "Where is my check, Mr. Taylor?"

A Racecar Instead of a Piano
I never was crazy about working fairs, although we worked at a lot of them in those early years. We were up in Ohio one time; I think it was in Watertown.

Now, my contract called for a piano to be provided and tuned to concert pitch, A=440. When we got there, I asked the fair manager, "Where's the piano?"

He said, "We don't got no piano."

I told him my contract called for a piano. He asked somebody standing there in the office, "Ain't we got a piano over there at the pack house? We did have at one time. Go over there and look at it."

So, we did, but it was tore all to pieces. We couldn't use it. We got set up and our bass guitar player just gave us the key for each song, "doom, doom, doom, doom," and that was all we had!

We started singing, and really, half the people didn't know the difference. If they weren't real dyed-in-the-wool quartet fans, you know, they didn't notice or care that anything was any different than usual.

To make matters worse, the racetrack was right beside where we were set up. Every time we'd get going, here would come a racecar around the track. They called them "hell cars" and buddy, that's a good name for them.

I don't think their boss man knew they were out there. Some of the drivers were just getting some practice, but I wished they hadn't done that while we were trying to sing. After the third or fourth time they came around, I told the crowd there, "If somebody will give me a rifle when he comes by again, I'll shoot the sucker."

After we got finished, the man in charge of the racetrack did come over and apologize to us. He said, "We had no idea anything was going on."

I will say this. When you're trying to sing "I'll Fly Away" and the piano you'd usually hear has been replaced by the sound of a "hell car" zooming by, it's going to sound rough!

They'll Go Further with Fuel in The Tank

Speaking of those "hell cars," there was another little venue we were in like that one time, and we got to know the guy that ran it pretty good. He had a growl in his voice when he talked. He told us, "I want you boys to be here tomorrow morning. I'm gonna show you some real hell driving."

Then he paused for emphasis and kind of swelled up and said, "I'm gonna drive one myself."

He was so persuasive that we made a point to show up the next morning and see exactly what he could do. He was a little guy about the size of McCray Dove, but a little thicker in the arms with his sleeves rolled up.

He got in that Mustang, revved it up, and took off down the track. What he was planning to do was come around and hit the railing and stay up on one side for a while, but that is not what really happened. What really happened was he got down around that first turn and came to a complete stop.

He got out of the car and came walking back. There was a small crowd there, but the stands were full. When he got close, we could hear him hollering out, "Who in the ____ was supposed to put gas in my car?"

I'm A Suit Collector

I guess you could call me a suit collector. My daughter Dara bought me a commercial rack for all the suits I've bought and saved over the years. I have 37 suits on that rack and probably 50 or more dress shirts. I never needed that many even when

I was still traveling. I bought some when we'd have the bus parked somewhere. I'd go to a store and shop just to have something to do.

Some of you might laugh about this, but I just about cried when Value City went out of business. That's where most of those suits came from. The best location I remember was in Huntington, West Virginia. In fact, I bought a bunch of sport coats there one day…maroon, black, blue, etc.

When JD Sumner's bus caught fire and destroyed a bunch of the clothes inside, I gave Rick Strickland his tenor singer some clothes I had bought up there. Every time I see Rick now, he still thanks me for those clothes.

A Different Cloud of Dust
Some of the singing we've done has been described as "three chords and a cloud of dust." People have used that phrase to describe the Kingsmen and the Happy Goodmans, too. I'm going to tell you about a cloud of dust of a different type.

Earlier in this book, I mentioned that my piano player for twelve years, Eric Ollis, would sometimes get so excited that he'd stand up, pull his coat off, and sling it out into the crowd. One of the first times he did that, I noticed a sort of brown cloud just floating in the air behind where he threw his coat.

What I haven't mentioned yet is that Eric was a snuff dipper at the time. He had a can of snuff in his coat pocket that came out, and boy, it went everywhere! I told Eric, "Man, don't ever do that again."

Tim Riley's Rug

A few years before we became the DMB Band, Gold City was just starting out. This was during the early 1980s. In the very beginning, Floyd Beck, who owned the group at the time, would call and ask promoters to let them open the show even if they wouldn't pay them any money. They were just happy to be getting their name out there.

When we shifted to the DMB Band and did the Christian Country style for a few years, I lost touch with what was going on in traditional Southern Gospel. During those same years, Gold City was stepping up to be one of the top male quartets in the entire business.

After I restarted with my traditional Dixie Melody Boys in 1987, the tables were turned on us. It was us who was opening concerts for groups like Gold City. We needed the exposure, and it was us who didn't always have much to show for it when we got back on the bus at the end of the day.

Before we got to know Gold City again, though, we'd been visiting in a home with some fans who had invited us to come over for snacks after a concert. There were some girls in that family who just loved Gold City. It was all they could talk about.

While we were there, they had a video of Gold City playing in one room, and I stepped in there to see what was going on. I watched the video for a minute. Sometimes I've been known to open my mouth and say something before I take enough time to think about it. I looked at the guys on the video and said, "Who is that old dude who looks like he's got a muskrat on his head?"

I was being serious. I really didn't know. When I'd seen their bass singer, Tim Riley, back in the early 1980s, he was bald headed. I didn't even realize it was the same guy.

Well, what I said made that girl mad, and I imagine she probably still wouldn't speak to me if she saw me today. Tim Riley sure is a good one, though; one of the absolute best.

Smoking

I'm not going to turn this into a tell-all about which popular singers smoked cigarettes, but without naming names, I will tell you about one member of another group who would hide his cigarettes on my bus. He did something I'll never forget.

When he'd get done smoking his cigarette in my room back there, he'd have a bottle of Mennen brand shaving lotion, the green kind. He'd dab it on his tongue and then slosh it around and spit.

He said if some of the female members of the group he was in knew he was smoking, they'd kill him! He later had some heart trouble and gave up smoking or at least, he said he did.

I knew another singer who had a fan who would bring him a black trash bag completely full of cartons of cigarettes every time he went to sing in that area of the country. Again, I'm not naming any names.

I can talk about this, because I was a smoker myself for a while. Back in those days, almost everyone smoked. I know a lot of preachers that smoked too.

The whole thing was just foolish of me. I'd made attempts to quit a few times. I'd tell my wife Joy I'd try to quit, or I'd cut down to just three a day, one after each meal. Before you know it, I'd be going back for another one, smoking more and more. If you're going to quit, cold turkey is the only way; at least it was for me. You've just got to make up your mind and quit, and that's what I did.

I was leaving the quartet convention one year when I was around thirty years old. I just had the thought, "This is the dumbest thing I've ever done. I've had to hide every time this week when I've decided to smoke a cigarette."

I ain't never smoked another one.

Fireworks!
Here are a few stories that have fireworks in common.

I was in the National Guard when I had the Gospel Harmony Quartet back in the 1950s. I bought a limousine from a funeral home to drive the group around to our singing dates in style, but I'd also drive it to Fort Bragg once a month for Guard meetings. I made a little money charging some other boys from the area who were in the National Guard five dollars per trip to ride with me.

We were all just young boys and cutting up most of the time. One day one of them had some firecrackers, and he decided to scare some people on the street. He lit one and leaned back to throw it out the window. Well, it hit the top of the door and bounced right back into the car between his legs. There was a scramble going on after it went off!

It didn't hurt nobody, but it scared us all including the guy who threw it. Those were the days.

Another story involves Claude Hopper. We've always been close friends. We started out about the same time, but I know Claude has made a lot more money doing this than me. In fact, when I told Claude I was thinking about writing this book, he said, "Man, I can't wait to read some of that stuff I know you're going to tell. I know some of it you can't tell, but what you can tell, I know it's gonna be funny."

Back in those early days, Claude and I both drove Eagle buses, and the thing about an Eagle is you have to put it on high idle when you stop so the oil will circulate and keep the engine cool. If you stop on low idle too many times, after a while, you're going to blow your engine.

We were at the Civic Center in Raleigh. The concert was over, and we had loaded up and everything. Claude had gone back in just to pick up something and come right back, so he didn't have his Eagle on high idle.

I had some of these little red smoke bombs. While Claude was in there, I got one of the boys to put one in the exhaust pipe and light it. When it started smoking, everybody started yelling, "Claude, Claude."

It tore Claude up and we all had a big laugh.

My last fireworks story involves my son Allen. Allen was my handyman when we were traveling. He's the kind of guy that if something happened to the bus, he could figure out how to get us home. He might have to rig it somehow to get it to run, but he'd get us home.

I had bought a generator so we could have lights inside the bus. It held about two quarts of oil and the manufacturer said it had to be changed every 100 hours. Allen kept up with it, and when that dial got to 100 hours, it didn't matter where we were, he had us pull over. It couldn't wait until we got to the auditorium, he wanted us to pull over right then. There were times when he even changed the oil in the generator with the bus sitting on the side of the interstate.

We had a boy who had just started playing drums at the time named Ricky. Ricky was so serious minded because he had just joined the group and he wanted to do right. Allen was unmerciful with Ricky playing jokes on him.

One night when we were getting ready to leave after a concert, I said, "Ricky, come in here. Now when everybody gets ready to get on the bus, you make sure you're the last one to get in. Light one of these smoke bombs and throw it in the bin where that generator is, and it will get Allen good."

Ricky said, "Oh no, I couldn't do that."

I finally talked him into it. I said, "Everybody will get a kick out of it. It'll make Allen mad, but don't worry about Allen. It'll be funny."

So, I made him do it. Ricky waited until everyone else was on the bus, set that smoke bomb off, threw it in the generator bin, and he got in.

We had wired the generator so it could be started from the back, or by pushing a button up front on the dash. I pushed the button, the generator started, and then I yelled, "Hey there's something smoking from that generator bin!"

Allen immediately jumped up and said, "Oh, my Lord."

Allen dashed off the bus and went back and reached in there to shut the generator off. With all the smoke pouring out, he couldn't see anything. He had to feel for the cutoff switch. As soon as he would find it and cut it off, I hit that button on the dash to start it up again. I did that three or four times, and every time he'd yell, "Cut it off!"

Ricky was afraid Allen was going to be so mad, but it all turned into a big joke.

We had a lot of fun. The younger the group, the more energy they have. They were always wanting to do something like that for a laugh.

Who Is It That Runs Peavey?

Speaking of my son Allen, he started riding with the group from the time he was in grammar grades in school. We started bringing him up to feature him on one song when he was still young. He's always had an interest in sound equipment.

We were in Freedom Hall in Louisville, Kentucky one year with the Hinsons and there were a bunch of other groups there as well. Now, I've always been a cut-up, and Ronny Hinson is a real cut-up too.

Allen had just got us a sponsorship from Peavey, a company that makes sound equipment down in Mississippi. They were furnishing sound for us and like I said, Allen was crazy over all that stuff. He was protective of it, too.

We got ready to go that night after the concert. I was driving a 45-foot GM bus at the time. We'd just loaded everything up, and Allen said we were ready to go. Now, I need to explain that back in those days, oil came in tin cans, not plastic. Ronny Hinson had observed just how serious Allen was about that Peavey sponsorship and how careful he was when it came to all the sound equipment.

Just before I backed up, Ronny Hinson put two or three of those tin oil cans behind our back wheels. I started backing out and heard them cans crushing. It made an awful racket. About that time Ronny yelled out, "Hey, whoa, whoa! Who is it that runs Peavey?"

Allen freaked out! He thought we had just destroyed our monitors. When you're traveling on the road, there are things that people do all the time like that just for a good laugh.

The DMB Band Made Good Courting Music
Earlier in this book in the chapter about the DMB Band, I mentioned I have a story about Sheri Easter. She was still named Sheri Lewis around the time I started shifting over to Christian Country music with the DMB Band.

Jeff Easter had asked Sheri out on a date, and when they were riding wherever they were going in the car, she was playing our tape *More Than Just Good Ole Boys*. One of the songs was called "Last Train to Glory." Jeff told Sheri he was playing on that tape. Well, Sheri didn't believe him. She just said, "Yeah, I bet you are."

Jeff said, "Well get the cover out."

Sure enough, his name was there in the credits along with all the other studio musicians. Jeff never was a member of the DMB Band, but he had come in to play harmonica when we recorded that album in the studio.

Jeff told me later that the fact he had played on the album gave him high marks with Sheri. I guess I get to take a little credit for their marriage working out as well as it did.

The Show Must Go On
We had a memorable performance at a fair in New York when Frank Sutton was singing tenor and playing bass guitar.

Frank had got a splinter stuck under his bass picking finger a few days before, and every time he picked a string, pain was shooting up his through his hand.

We built up to a big finish on our last song, "How Great Thou Art." The crowd was loving it when we hit that final chord, but I didn't hear a tenor singer or a bass guitar.

When he went to hit the last note, Frank had leaned way back like Archie Watkins and picked that bass guitar string extra hard. It caused so much pain that he passed out cold. To make matters worse, the crowd thought it was all part of the act!

My son Allen was playing rhythm guitar right behind Frank and managed to slow his fall as he leaned backwards and collapsed. Meanwhile, the concert promoter saw the crowd applauding and motioned for us to sing another song.

I knew we couldn't sing anything else without a tenor or a bass guitar player, so I did the only thing I could think to do in the moment. I stood over Frank as he lay there in pain, and I went into my record pitch!

Another situation where the show must go on is when you get delayed on the way to a concert. One time we were in New England for an afternoon singing. I think we'd already sung a concert that morning. Rayburn Lane was driving the bus, and we were going down to get on the big highway. A lady clipped us, and that made us late getting to the concert.

By the time we finally did get to the church, it was packed. I said, "Boys, we can't set up now. We ain't got time. Let's walk in singing a cappella all the way down the aisle to the platform, and then we'll just choose some songs."

That just thrilled those people to death. I think they probably enjoyed seeing us make the best of the situation more than they would if we had set up our sound system and sang all of our regular material.

Another time we were at a Catholic church in Louisville, Kentucky. They'd just spent 3.5 million dollars renovating this big sanctuary. They had a concert series. Every night was a different style, and why they wanted us, I'll never know, but the Harper Agency booked us in there for a big amount of money. We started setting up the sound system, and I said, "Boys, that ain't gonna work."

Everything was marble…floors, walls, and ceiling. So, we tried one a cappella and decided that was the only way to do it. Of course, they weren't used to our style of music. We'd finish a song and they'd clap, but it was the soft, polite kind of clapping like they were at a Broadway show or something.

When we got through, the lady handed me a check, and she said, "Oh, that was fantastic. You guys were just fantastic!"

I asked her who they were bringing in the next day for their concert series, and she said, "Oh, we've got the Franciscan monks coming. They're going to chant for us."

That was unusual.

We were in Richmond, Virginia the last time I remember us having one of those moments where we had to improvise so the concert could continue. The power went out and the emergency lights came on. We sang the rest of that concert a cappella by those lights.

My Granddaddy's Oranges

Now I'm going to take you back to my childhood and tell you a funny story about my granddaddy on my mother's side of the family. Oranges were a rare treat in those days. They would get a few around Christmas. Of course, if anyone came to their house to visit, they felt obligated to share. It's just the kind of thing neighbors did back in those days.

When company came over to visit in the home, they would usually show up unannounced. Many people had no way to call ahead even if they wanted to. Telephones weren't in every house back in those days.

My granddaddy lived about a quarter of a mile off the main highway down a dirt path. He knew when a car was coming down his driveway before it got there, because he could see a big plume of dust rising in the air.

My grandma's name was Lennie. I remember Granddaddy seeing a car coming one day, and he yelled, "Lennie, hide the oranges! Here comes Mr. so-and-so and the whole d___ family."

Granddaddy never was in a sharing mood when it came to his oranges. I have laughed every time I've thought about that incident now for almost 80 years!

Turtles Bite Hard!
Old people were funny to me when I was a kid. I loved to just sit around and listen to them talk. I never did know my granddaddy on my father's side of the family. He passed away before I could get to know him, but I do remember my daddy telling about a time he went squirrel hunting with my granddaddy.

After they'd been out for a while, they sat down to rest a little bit. They noticed a turtle sitting there on the ground, so my granddaddy started messing with it. The next thing he knew it had bit his finger and it wouldn't let go!

Now he'd always heard if a turtle bites you, it won't let go until it hears thunder. He said, "Sonny, get over there behind that log and make a thunder sound!"

My daddy said this was the truth. He said he got over there and made some loud rumbling sounds like thunder and then my granddaddy hollered, "You better quit; it's hurtin' worse!"

A Ford Can Scare You If You've Never Seen One Before
Another story my daddy told me was about the first time they ever saw an automobile. He and his sister were over in the field doing something, and they heard a rumbling sound unlike anything they had ever heard before.

They thought the world was coming to an end and that the Lord was about to come back right then or maybe it was the devil coming to get them. He said they went and hid behind a bunch of rocks and stuff. It kept getting closer and closer until here come a little A-model Ford. It was the first car they'd ever seen.

Can you imagine what that would be like if you'd never seen a car or anything like it before? Their whole life up until that moment, their whole concept of transportation was limited to riding horses and mules.

Some of the old-timers really were superstitious, too. They thought you could get rid of warts by throwing a dishrag under the house and walking around the house three times.

It was a different time, for sure.

Short Tenures
When Rodney Griffin came up with the idea for Ed O'Neal University, our tenor singer at that time, Matt Felts, helped create a shirt with about 45 or 50 of the former members' names on the back of it. We were doing a reunion event in Pigeon Forge at the National Quartet Convention on Saturday afternoon when my son Allen saw the shirt. He said, "You're missing a bunch of them."

Allen started naming names and I think we eventually came up with 90 former members. It is no secret that I've had more group members come and go over the years than anyone else in this business. Some of the boys who sang with the Dixie

Melody Boys were only with us for a short time. I was doing an interview the other day, and a guy asked me if I could remember the shortest length of time somebody had stayed with the group. I said, "One day."

We hired a guy and seemed to get along fine. He did a great job on his first day working at my annual homecoming at the ball stadium there.

We were scheduled to sing in a church the next morning. I went through the bus to get everybody up, but he was not in his bunk. We looked in his closet and found his suit hanging in there along with the shoes I'd bought him. Everything else of his was gone.

I still to this day haven't heard a thing as to why he left!

Short People Can Sleep Anywhere
If you ride around in a bus long enough, you're going to find yourself sitting on the side of the road broken down sooner or later. What buses are guaranteed to do is break down.

When (not if) the bus breaks down, my top priority is to stay calm and collected. I try not to get too flustered or too upset about it. Once you accept the fact that all buses new or old are guaranteed to break down sooner or later, you learn to deal with it without pitching a fit.

My next step is to figure out where I can rent a van and trailer to get to the next date. I never want to disappoint the people who have contracted me to come sing. Once that is settled, I can then move on to getting the bus running again.

Back when McCray Dove was traveling with us, we had bus trouble more than a few times. Everyone would try to find a place to rest on those rented van seats. One day I couldn't find McCray. I didn't see him laying down on any of the seats, and I was worried we might have driven off and left him the last time we'd stopped for gas.

Keep in mind that McCray is barely five feet tall and back then he probably weighed no more than 125 pounds soaking wet. A little fellow like that is easy to misplace.

I finally found him curled up and fast asleep. He was laying UNDER the front passenger seat of the van.

Jerry Kelso
The first bus I ever had with a professional interior was a GM. I was tickled to death over that bus, except the trash can in the lounge area sat in a drawer with a mechanism that should have latched to keep it closed. The latch was broken, so the trash can was constantly flopping back and forth every time we went around a curve on the road.

My piano player Jerry Kelso was always reading when he was with us and mostly from the Bible. I was driving, and Jerry was up on the couch over to the side studying his Bible. Meanwhile, the sound of that trash can flopping was getting on my nerves.

My son Allen had been putting his overnight bag in front of it to hold it in place, but he was back in the back. I said, "Jerry, don't you hear that drawer slamming back and forth?"

He said, "I hadn't really noticed it."

I said, "Well, go get a bag and put in front of it."

Jerry went to the back of the bus, and this is the truth if I ever told it. He came back up front with a Walmart bag and pressed it out flat on the floor. Then he sat back down and went back to reading his Bible.

I didn't say nothing else. I just kept driving, and that trash can kept on flopping!

First Impressions Aren't Always Accurate
We did a concert one time at Carowinds which is a big theme park just south of Charlotte on the North Carolina/South Carolina state line. Jim Bakker had bought out the whole place for a day so all his employees and their families could enjoy the park.

We came in to be part of a concert that also included Dave Boyer, the Happy Goodman Family, and some guy named Carman. I'd never heard of Carman before.

Dave Boyer was on first, then the Dixie Melody Boys, and then the Goodmans. I told one of the boys, "Man, they're saving that little fellow for last."

He was wearing a golf shirt, khaki pants, and loafers with no socks. I wondered, "What's that little fellow gonna do?"

Carman went out there and started up a track and started in to singing. It was not bad, but I didn't think it was that good either. I really felt sorry for him. He was following the Happy Goodmans which is no easy task, and to me he seemed like just an OK singer.

All of a sudden, he started that song, "Lazarus, Come Forth" and the whole place just came unglued. The entire crowd was standing up cheering by the end of it. It was then that I knew my first impression of this little guy had led me wrong.

Carman got that crowd's attention in a way I'd never have imagined based on what I first saw and heard. He's built on it ever since. My former tenor singer Matt Felts works as Carman's manager now.

The Devil's on the Front Row
When I restarted the Dixie Melody Boys as a traditional quartet in the late 1980s, McCray Dove was still a teenager and all the other boys in the group were probably under the age of 25. I let them have some fun when we were on the bus, but I expected them to be professionals on stage and I let them know it.

McCray says it was hard sometimes to maintain composure. He says I would turn around sometimes and say something to them on stage that would get them so tickled, they could hardly sing.

One night there was a young woman who came to our concert who didn't have on enough clothes to be seen in a Walmart, much less a gospel singing. Keep in mind that all my boys on stage were in their late teens or early twenties at that time.

I knew they had all noticed her immediately, because she was sitting right there on the front row where she couldn't be missed. If she'd picked anywhere else to sit, she might not have been as much of a distraction, but she was sitting on the front row!

After we'd sung our first song, I turned around away from the mic and said soft enough the audience couldn't hear but loud enough for my boys to hear, "You better keep your eyes on Jesus, boys, because the devil is sitting on the front row!"

McCray tells that story sometimes now. He says they all could hardly sing for laughing all the way through the next song on the program.

Will the Circle Be Unbroken?
I've learned over the years when a crowd is a little too quiet, that taking a few requests can help get them involved. We were in Maryland one time at a church that seated about 500 and it seemed like 600 were trying to get in. It was a large crowd, but all we were getting was a little bit of soft, polite clapping after we had sung each song.

I said, "We'd like to take a few of your requests."

A lady a few rows back said, "Oh, I'd love to hear you sing 'Will the Circle Be Unbroken.' "

This was when Dan Keeton was singing tenor and Andrew King was singing baritone and picking bass guitar. None of them really knew the song well enough to sing it other than me, but as I was turning to get the key, Andrew said, "I've got it."

Andrew took off singing, "I remember when I was a lad, times were hard…"

He was thinking of "Daddy Sang Bass," because it includes part of "Will the Circle Be Unbroken" at the end. I looked over at Dan Keeton and said, "You get to be Mama."

Dan said, "I ain't singing."

Andrew was so embarrassed when he realized what he'd done. What a time, what a time!

The Strangest Thing I Ever Saw
We were singing at a concert in Kempton, Pennsylvania with the Hemphills one night and had parked our buses around behind the stage. One woman acted kind of crazy and was smoking cigarettes while we were singing. I thought, "This is very unusual."

After it was over and we were packed up and ready to leave, she fell out on the ground having convulsions right in front of my bus. Her head was right behind the front wheel.

The Hemphills said she had a demon in her. LaBreeska said to let Joel work with her, because she'd seen this before. Now, I was wanting to leave, because we needed to get on the road to go to Ohio for our next date, but there was nothing I could do with her laying there.

We finally got her up and she was cussing like a sailor. Joel and LaBreeska were saying "Jesus, Jesus, Jesus" over her.

Whether it was a true demon possession or just a put-on, I don't know, but she would take a swing at LaBreeska with her fist, and it would bounce to one side or the other like there was an invisible shield blocking her from making contact. I thought, "This is kind of strange, and I really do need to get out of here."

But we just had to wait until she got up. That's probably the strangest thing I've ever seen in all my years out on the road.

I saw something similar one time when we were singing at a camp-meeting up in Ypsilanti, Michigan outside under a tent. A lady fired up a cigarette about four or five rows back, I guess to see if she could attract some attention. Of course, she did, and when they tried to get her out, it caused a big scene.

Mel McDaniel's Bus
We were booked to perform for an annual celebration at the courthouse in Newton, North Carolina a few years ago. That same day, just a few miles down the road in Maiden, North Carolina, we picked up a new bus that I had just purchased from Goodson Bus Sales.

It was a beautiful coach that had previously been owned by the Nashville country music star Mel McDaniel. We picked up the coach that morning, drove it around a while, and then went to lunch. After that, we decided to go on down to the courthouse to park and get some rest. It was around 2 o'clock in the afternoon when we arrived.

We always had a good crowd for this event, but most years in the past they were contained in the courthouse grounds. That day I noticed some people had already started coming at 3 o'clock. By 5 o'clock the grounds around the courthouse were full and people kept on coming with their folding chairs. I've never seen a promoter so excited.

The police finally came and closed all the streets so the people could set their chairs out there. By the time the concert started, chairs full of people were all the way across the street and pushed up against the storefronts. The promoter said he had never seen a crowd that big, and we were getting all of the credit for drawing those people!

We finally realized the reason. My new bus had been parked in the street since 2 o'clock, and that beautiful coach still had Mel McDaniel's name on it. Word got around the community quickly and the people just assumed Mel McDaniel was there to perform. I guess some people were terribly disappointed, but boy, what a night! People still talk about the night.

While I still had that bus that had belonged to Mel McDaniel, I hired a new driver. It was a beautiful bus inside, and it had a "star" room in the back with a big bed in it. That's where I slept, or at least, that's where I tried to sleep.

I thought my new driver did pretty good down around Greensboro and up toward Asheville. When we got up in the gorge on I-40 past Asheville going into Tennessee through all those curves, though, I started rolling into the wall. First, I'd roll to one side and then I'd roll over to the other side. I thought, "Good gracious, what is going on up there?"

I got up and went up front. He was hitting 70 miles an hour through those curves! The bus was leaning one way and then it would lean the other way. I said, "Buddy, how about slowing it down!"

Now let me make it clear right quick that this bus driver I'm talking about was not my long-time driver, Rayburn Lane. Rayburn is one of my best friends, and he is a smooth driver, too. A few years ago, when Rayburn was driving the bus for the Dove Brothers, he had a bumper sticker on the back of the bus that said, "I'm hauling people, not potatoes."

Singers need a good night's rest so we can give it our all when we get to the next concert. Potatoes don't care. A great bus driver knows how to ease into a curve or slow down if he sees a bump ahead in the road. A driver who only thinks about getting there in the least amount of time possible might make a good potato hauler, but he'll be a sorry bus driver.

I heard about another group owner who had a rough trip one weekend due to hiring one of those potato haulers to drive his bus. When they finished up the trip and made it back home, he paid the man and said, "I hope you enjoy this check I'm giving you, because it's the last one you'll ever get from me."

Gen'lly Speaking

Speaking of Rayburn Lane, let me tell you about a time when he almost got arrested. We were on our way to Jacksonville, Florida, and it was one of those trips that was going to take all night to get there. I drove first and then Rayburn took over around three o'clock in the morning. I told him I wanted to sleep and not to wake me up until an hour or so before we needed to set up our equipment.

There's a certain motion you get used to when you sleep on a bus, and I was resting comfortably. When we got down near the Gator Bowl stadium, though, it changed to the stop-and-go motion of a traffic jam. We finally stopped completely.

I went up to see what was going on. There I found Rayburn speaking to what I am sure was one of the great City of Jacksonville's finest police officers. He'd pulled us over to ask why our bus was holding up traffic. I haven't mentioned this yet, but this officer was small in stature. He also seemed to be the sort of policeman who took his job a little too seriously.

He said to Rayburn, "This thoroughfare is not on the way to your destination. Why are you interfering with the traffic flow of this area?"

Rayburn drawled, "Sir, I'm sorry. Gen'lly speaking, we never come this way."

The officer snapped back, "What did you call me?"

Rayburn said, "I didn't call you anything. I just said gen'lly speaking, we never come this way."

The officer said, "You just called me a general, didn't you? Are you making fun of me because you're taller? Are you going to call me 'General Napoleon' now? Would you like to inspect the inside of a police car?"

Rayburn said, "No, I said, gen'lly speaking…"

The officer interrupted, "Boy, don't you call me that again!"

"I didn't call you anything. Gen'lly speaking, we always take…"

"I told you not to call me that! I'll have you off that bus and into a cell before you can count to five!"

I was practically laying down on the floor of the bus by now, because I was laughing so hard. Rayburn was getting madder by the minute, both at the officer and because he could hear me laughing behind him.

After they argued for what seemed like 10 minutes, he was finally able to convince the officer he wasn't making fun of him. The officer finally allowed us to go on our way.

Rayburn may have been rid of the officer that day, but he wasn't rid of me. Every time I spoke to Rayburn for the rest of the day, I'd say something like, "How's it going, gen'lly speaking?" or, "What did you do today, gen'lly speaking?" or, "Gen'lly speaking, Jacksonville's got some great police officers, don't they?"

Rayburn stayed mad at me for a week or more.

Another Encounter with Law Enforcement
For the past few years, we have traveled in a Sprinter van. Even if you have a great driver, a Sprinter will not ride as smoothly as a bus. Sometimes we would schedule time in our trips to stop at a campground to have time to get some rest.

We had stopped at a campground in Georgia a few years ago. After we were settled in, our baritone Steven Cooper walked around through the campground trying to find a signal for his cell phone. Out near the front of the park, he found a picnic table where the reception was better, so he sat there to make his call.

My tenor singer Jonathan Price and my lead singer Donald Morris noticed a deep ditch that ran close to the picnic table. They thought it would be funny to sneak up that ditch close to Steven and then jump out to scare him. As they both crawled into the ditch, they were thinking about the look that would be on Steven's face when they came up out of there screaming at the top of their lungs.

As they went into the ditch, though, they didn't notice a police car easing up behind them! The policeman naturally thought they must be up to something worse than a harmless prank.

It took them both a while to convince the deputy they were just trying to scare Steven. In fact, Steven had to help them out a bit by explaining he knew who they were.

They're just lucky it wasn't me out there instead of Steven. I would have said, "I've never seen either one of those boys in my entire life!"

Harold Refuses to Sleep
One year when we were on our annual west coast tour, the great Southern Gospel pioneer James Blackwood was riding on our bus. We decided to stop for something to eat, but we wanted to keep moving, so we just went into a convenience store to pick up a few items. I got saltine crackers and a can of Beanie-Weenies. James came out with an egg salad sandwich and some potato chips.

Harold Reed was the tenor singer for the Dixie Melody Boys at that time. Harold was the type who usually headed straight for his bunk after a concert. This night, though, I noticed he stayed up front with us.

As we started eating our snacks, James Blackwood started telling us stories about his career as a gospel singer from the early days: the big concerts they appeared on in Long Beach, California; the plane crash in Clanton, Alabama that claimed the lives of Blackwood Brothers singers Bill Lyles and R W Blackwood as well as the plane's pilot and another friend in 1954; what Hovie, Jake, and Big Chief were like in the early days, and so much more. James was still talking when the sun came up the next morning!

I was most surprised that Harold never had gone to bed because he was always one of those "early to bed" types like I mentioned. At one point, Harold looked over at me and said, "Wow."

I said, "What do you mean?"

He said, "James Blackwood is on our bus, eating an egg salad sandwich. This is heaven on earth! Wow!"

That boy had his priorities in the right order.

Tony Brown Couldn't Stop Laughing
Tony Brown had claustrophobia when he was with us. This was just after I first started singing with the Dixie Melody Boys.

The bus we had did not have a professional interior. We just installed bunks in there and did what we could to customize it ourselves. We had painted the windows in the back black to keep it dark so we could sleep. Over Tony's bunk, though, we had to scrape that black paint back off. Tony would go crazy if he couldn't see outside.

Tony was just seventeen or eighteen years old at the time he was with us. Like a lot of young boys at that age, he was a giggler. Everything was funny to him. You never knew what might set him off laughing, and whenever he did get tickled, you wondered if he ever would quit laughing!

We were at a big fancy church in Washington, DC one Sunday sitting on the front row waiting on the minister (whose first name had "Doctor" in front of it) to call us up to sing. He came out real sophisticated and said, "Ladies and gentlemen, we're so glad to have the Dixie Melody Boys here this morning. They blessed us last time, and I'm sure they will again today. But before they come up to sing, brother so-and-so is going to render a special song for us."

The young man who went up to sing looked like a banker with a nice suit on and shiny shoes. He got up and took his podium and positioned it over in the front, then he took out his sheet music and licked his thumb and turned it over.

After he was all set, he looked over at the lady at the piano and cleared his throat, "Ahem," to give her the signal he was ready to begin. The piano player rolled a chord and he started his song: "Colored folks work on the Mississippi…" (He was singing "Ol' Man River!")

Tony got so tickled, we had to take him out of there and get him settled down before we went back in to sing. He just couldn't quit laughing once he got started.

We Had the Tigers by the Tail
We were on a program with JD Sumner & the Stamps Quartet at the Masonic Temple in Detroit, Michigan in 1984 when the Detroit Tigers baseball team was headed to the World Series. It was all anybody in that town was talking about.

I was sitting there on the bus thinking about it and got an idea. I gave my son Allen some money and said, "Go somewhere and buy me four Detroit Tigers ball caps."

Allen said, "What are you gonna do?"

I said, "I've just got an idea."

Well, they went and got them and brought them back. So, when they introduced the Dixie Melody Boys on the program that night, we walked out with them ball caps on and sang, "Take Me Out to The Ballgame." The place just came apart.

After our set was over, JD had to follow that. He said, "You're a dirty man, Ed. I've seen it all now."

JD Sets His Own Sound

We were singing on a program in Kempton, Pennsylvania on hired sound, so we didn't have to set up any of our speakers. JD Sumner & The Stamps were on the same program, but JD said, "I'm singing on my own sound, or I'm not singing."

He sent his tenor singer, Rick Strickland, out to tell the sound guy in the house. That guy told Rick that it was not allowed. JD himself got off the bus at that point, and before it was settled, they had a big fuss. They finally agreed JD could mix his own monitors to control the sound on stage, but the sound man would control the levels heard by the audience.

At the end of the program, JD said to the audience, "Before we go, I just want to say what a blessing your sound man has been to me."

As far as the crowd knew, JD and the sound man were best buddies. They didn't know the two of them had been at each other's throats before the show started.

JD and WB
Speaking of sound systems, let me tell you one about WB Nowlin who promoted a lot of big concerts in Texas. I loved him to death. He was instrumental in promoting the Happy Goodmans in their heyday and many other top groups. WB was also known for the series of concerts he called the Battle of Songs.

When WB was getting on up in years, we'd go in along with three or four groups like the Stamps and the Florida Boys. Each group would set up their own sound system.

Before one event where we were working for WB with JD Sumner & The Stamps, WB said, "Why in the world do you do this? I used to have Eddy Arnold come in, and they'd fill the auditorium with one little sound system. Now you've got to have all that sound and it's so loud. I can't even give away a ticket! Why don't you tie all your sound systems together?"

JD said, "WB, that is a good idea."

So, JD sent Ed Hill or somebody down to the hardware store and got a bundle of rope. He came back and ran that rope around through the speaker stands, "tying them together."

JD always loved to mess with WB, but they were also great friends! We used to sing at the music hall in Houston, and the next night we'd be at Will Rogers Auditorium in Fort Worth. WB would usually make the ride over on JD's bus. He loved JD.

One year we followed them along in our buses, and they stopped to eat at a little pancake house somewhere between Houston and Fort Worth. Now, WB was allergic to dairy products, so he didn't want butter anywhere near his food.

JD knew this. We went on into the restaurant and everybody went to sit down, but JD kind of lingered behind and told the waitress, "When that old man orders, he's gonna order a waffle, and he really don't want butter on it, but I want you to put a fistful on it!"

She started to protest to JD, "Oh no, I could never do anything like that."

JD said, "It's gonna be a joke. It'll be funny. Everybody will get a great big laugh from it."

So, to get her to do it, JD gave her a $20.00 bill.

We all placed our orders and after a while it came out. I got my eggs and bacon and each of the other men got his order.

When she set that waffle down in front of WB with that big wad of butter in the middle, he immediately began to protest, "Hunh uh! Honey, honey, honey, come back here! I can't eat that with that butter! I can't have the butter."

She said, "I'll scrape it off."

WB, clearly upset, shot back, "No, you won't either! You'll cook me another one!"

Well, JD just mouthed to her real soft where WB couldn't hear, "Do it again."

She did that three times and the third time, WB flung the plate across the floor and said, "I told you I couldn't have butter!"

That JD was a mess.

The last time I saw WB before he passed away, I was staying at the Hyatt Regency. My wife Joy and I were going in and I saw him riding the trolley. I told her to go on in and I'd get on the trolley, because I thought he might be disoriented and not sure where to get off. I sat down beside him and said, "How are you WB?"

We talked while we rode down to Municipal Hall where most everyone got off, but he didn't get off there. We came back to the Hyatt and he was in the middle of telling a story, so we stayed on and made another round trip. After about three times around, WB looked at me and said, "When in the devil am I going to get to my room?"

He was staying at the Hyatt too, so I helped him find where he was going. WB was such a good guy.

JD Loses A Bet

Like I mentioned in the first chapter of this book, JD Sumner always was my hero, and then he became my pal. We played a lot of golf together.

We were playing in Nashville one day with Jack Bagwell who sang many years with the Palmetto State Quartet. There was one more with us that day, too, but I can't remember who it was.

Now Jack Bagwell was a good golfer. When we got on the number 16 tee box, Jack looked at JD and said, "JD, I thought you were a better golfer than what you've been today."

JD said, "Well, I don't have no incentive. There ain't nothing riding on it. You want to bet something?"

Jack said, "It's up to you."

JD shot back, "You name it, pal."

Jack suggested, "Well, we have 16, 17, and 18 to go. Let's go $100 a hole."

JD said, "You're on. Hit it."

Then JD proceeded to lose every hole.

I was riding with him. We went back to the car and put our clubs in the back. When we got in and took off, he turned to the right. I said, "JD, you're going the wrong way. We came in from the left."

I could tell it irritated him a little bit because he raised his voice and growled, "I'm going to the bank to get Jack his money, OK?"

Glen Payne Sells One Album
Glen Payne was another one of my best friends. This story is not anything I saw myself, but Glen told me about it. He said The Cathedrals really struggled for a while after they left Rex Humbard's Cathedral of Tomorrow to venture out on their own.

Glen said during those years they went to one Saturday night concert in Fort Worth, Texas, and all they sold was one album to a little old lady. Just one.

That's not the worst of it, though. The next day on Sunday morning they were at a Baptist church in Dallas, and that same little old lady came to see them again. After it was over, she came up to their table carrying that record she had bought in Fort Worth, and she wanted Glen to give her money back!

I Ain't Singing Baritone
Since I'm telling about Glen, I may as well tell you what George Younce did to me one year at Christmas. He called me on Christmas Day, and after we'd wished each other a Merry Christmas and everything, George said, "Oh, by the way,

there's a trio trying to get started up here in Stow, Ohio, and wanted me to ask you if you'd be interested in singing baritone."

I guess George thought that was funny, but I didn't see much humor in it. I ain't singing baritone for nobody!

Are You Ed O'Neal?
JD Sumner was my buddy and believe it or not, some people got us confused from time to time. If you saw us apart, I suppose we looked similar, but if you saw us together, we didn't look alike at all. He was taller than I was, and his features and hands were huge.

One time when the Stamps had stopped at a filling station in Little Rock, Arkansas, Ed Hill was driving the bus. JD said, "Ed, I'm going to go in and get some breakfast. You come on in after you get the bus filled up with fuel."

They were sitting there eating breakfast, and a lady thought she recognized JD. She stopped and touched him on the shoulder and said, "Excuse me, sir, but are you Ed O'Neal?"

When Ed Hill told me about that later, he laughed and said it made JD so mad. He said JD looked at that lady and growled, "No, I'm not!"

He put a big pause after each of his initials as he said to her, "My name is J.. D.. Sumner!"

Are you JD Sumner?

It happened to me, too. McCray Dove sat up with me a lot when I would drive the bus. We'd been on a long haul one night and stopped in Athens, Tennessee. We stopped at a little restaurant there to eat breakfast.

A middle-aged lady approached our table to take our order, and I noticed she kept looking at me like she recognized me. After a while she said, "Are you JD Sumner?"

I said, "No Ma'am."

She kept on writing on the order pad, and then she said, "Are you sure you're not JD Sumner?"

McCray said softly, "Tell her, Ed."

And then he said to the waitress, "Yes, he's JD."

She was crying when she turned and left to go turn in the order. When she came back, I noticed up on her lapel she had Elvis Presley pins. The next time she came back, she had a portfolio of pictures that she put on the table of the inside of her house. The whole basement of her house was wall-to-wall, just solid with Elvis stuff.

I'll never forget McCray doing that, telling that lady I was JD, but I guess it made her day!

(left to right) Ed O'Neal, Jerry Kelso, and JD Sumner

My name is Ed O'Neal. I'm 84 years old, and all I've ever wanted to do is sing a song.

Made in the USA
Columbia, SC
04 November 2020